Monday Night
ZARAHEMLA

M000007504

To my children—
you inspire me.

Monday Nights in

ZARAHEMLA

32 Lessons and Games for Family Home Evening
Based on the Book of Mormon

by Janet Burningham

CFI
Springville, Utah

©2007 Janet Burningham

All rights reserved.

No part of this book may be reproduced in any form whatsoever, whether by graphic, visual, electronic, film, microfilm, tape recording, or any other means without prior written permission of the author, except in the case of brief passages embodied in critical reviews and articles.

This is not an official publication of The Church of Jesus Christ of Latter-day Saints. The opinions and views expressed herein belong solely to the author and do not necessarily represent the opinions or views of Cedar Fort, Inc. Permission for the use of sources, graphics, and photos is also solely the responsibility of the author.

ISBN: 978-1-59955-127-2

Published by Cedar Fort, Inc.
2373 W. 700 S., Springville, Utah, 84663
www.cedarfort.com
Distributed by Cedar Fort

LIBRARY OF CONGRESS CATALOGING-IN-PUBLICATION DATA

Burningham, Janet.
  Family home evening with the Book of Mormon : lessons to help your family
learn and apply important truths from the Book of Mormon / Janet Burningham.
    p. cm.
  ISBN 978-1-59955-127-2 (alk. paper)
  1. Book of Mormon—Criticism, interpretation, etc. 2. Family—Religious
life. I. Title.

  BX8627.B844 2007
  289.3'2207—dc22

                                    007042821

Cover design by Nicole Williams
Edited and typeset by Kimiko M. Hammari
Cover design © 2007 by Lyle Mortimer
Illustrations © 2007 by Spencer Wood

Printed in the United States of America
10 9 8 7 6 5 4 3 2 1

Printed on acid-free paper

CONTENTS

APPENDIX

INTRODUCTION

This book is designed to make family home evening and studying the Book of Mormon easier and more enjoyable for families. There are thirty-two lessons on well-known stories and topics in the Book of Mormon as well as games to help enrich your family's learning. The lessons in this book will help develop better comprehension and application of the important truths taught in the scriptures.

The stories and topics in this guide are arranged chronologically but may be studied in any order. Each time you gather together for family home evening, select a story or topic to read and discuss. Depending on how much time you wish to spend, you could cover an entire lesson, or just part of a lesson; do whatever is best for your family. Most lessons cover an average of thirty verses. For younger children, this may be too much to read at one time. In our home, I check off the verses we have read, and the next time we start where we left off.

It's true that family home evening and studying the scriptures can often be a struggle for families. I have experienced this in my own home. I also know

that the effort it takes is well worth it.

Reading the scriptures together should never be a stressful or rushed experience. Always remember that love and kindness should prevail, and try to ensure that the Spirit is present during this important teaching time.

It is our responsibility as parents to teach our children the ways of God. I know if we have faith, He will help us keep His commandments. We can all learn from Nephi's example when he says, "I will go and do the things which the Lord has commanded, for I know that the Lord giveth no commandments unto the children of men, save he shall prepare a way for them that they may accomplish the thing which he commandeth them" (1 Nephi 3:7).

I have a strong testimony of the importance of family home evening and of reading the scriptures as a family. By doing so, children can better understand the language, the stories, the principles of the gospel, and how to apply them in their lives. Above all else, studying the scriptures will help them gain a testimony of Jesus Christ.

HOW TO USE THIS BOOK

Hi! My name is Simeon, and I am a scripture guide. I will be with you as you journey through the Book of Mormon. The Book of Mormon was written by prophets over a thousand years ago, and sometimes it is hard to understand. But don't let that discourage you, because I am here to help!

There are thirty-two lessons in this guide, along with charts, maps, and explanations that can help you better understand the Book of Mormon. You will find the following sections in each lesson:

BACKGROUND INFORMATION

Before beginning each lesson, make sure you read the background information. Here you will find information about who you will be reading about. You will also be reminded of other people and stories that are connected to the one you will be reading.

GOSPEL ART PICTURE KIT

Each lesson has a reference to the Church's Gospel Art Picture Kit that corresponds well with the lesson. Using visual aids can help children better relate to the lesson and retain information they have studied.

WORD QUEST

Learning the language of the scriptures is very important in understanding them. At the beginning of each lesson you will find a list of words. You might want to assign a word or two to each person in your family before you begin. Each person is responsible for looking for their word while you read. When you get to each word, stop and talk about the meaning. Easy-to-understand definitions for each word are given at the right side of the page under "Treasures of Knowledge." There's also a glossary in the back of the book where you can keep track of the new words and their definitions.

VERSES / SUGGESTED QUESTIONS

A series of simple comprehension and application questions are provided with each section of verses. There are several ways in which the verses can be studied: (1) Read the questions before reading the verses. Some children (especially younger children) may benefit from having the questions given to them before they read a particular verse. This gives them something to look for when they read and helps them understand what they read. (2) Read each section of verses like it is shown. Then stop to read the corresponding questions. This helps ensure the children are comprehending what they are reading. (3) Read through all the verses listed, and then go back and read the questions. (Note: The verses in which the answers can be found are given in parentheses next to the questions. Older children might prefer reading all of the verses first and answering the questions later—especially if you plan to play a game that includes questions from the lesson.)

Sometimes the study guide skips around within the chapter or chapters being studied and does not include every verse. Please feel free to include any other verses, or discuss additional questions that you feel are appropriate for your family. Remember these are only suggestions; what's important is that you find a method that works well for your family.

TREASURES OF KNOWLEDGE

The lesson table includes a column with comments or explanations that may further enhance your understanding of the scriptural passage just read. The definitions for the words listed in the Word Quest are also found here.

APPENDIX

Lehi's Journey: Use this map when you are studying the lessons related to Lehi and his family. It will help you visualize where they traveled. (Note: No one knows for sure where Lehi landed on the American continent.)

Chart of Nephite Leaders: This will help you see who is related to whom. Each time you learn about someone for the first time, be sure to locate him on this chart.

Book of Mormon Cities: This map shows possible sites for cities that are studied in this guide, along with an explanation of who occupied those cities. There are several stories in the Book of Mormon that take place at the same time. This map and explanation should help you understand where the Nephites lived in relation to one another.

Who's Who in the Book of Mormon: This section lists and describes people in the Book of Mormon stories that are studied in this guide. It includes where and when they lived, along with a brief synopsis of their lives.

Word Quest Glossary: This glossary includes all the words from each Word Quest. No definitions are given here; this is where the children write down the definitions as they learn them. By having the children write the definitions down themselves, it will help the children to remember them better.

Games, Games, Games!: This section contains thirty-two fun family activities that require little or no preparation and can be played with any lesson. There are games that help increase comprehension by using questions from the lessons, games that help teach and reinforce Book of Mormon knowledge, and games just for fun. Most games can be adapted to fit both older and younger children.

WHAT IS THE BOOK OF MORMON?

Did you know that the Book of Mormon is the true record of an ancient people who lived hundreds of years ago on the American continent?

The Lord commanded many of the prophets and kings who lived during that time to write a history of their people. These histories were written on metal plates and passed down from one generation to another.

The prophet Mormon was one of the last people to keep a story of his life. Mormon was also given the other histories that the previous kings and prophets had kept since Lehi and Nephi (over one thousand year's worth of records!).

There were so many plates that the Lord commanded Mormon to read through all the stories and write a shorter history of the people on gold plates. God helped Mormon and told him what parts to include in his writings.

The first six books in the Book of Mormon are the small plates of Nephi—a record written by the prophet Nephi and his descendants. These books are written in first person. God told Mormon to include these plates in the writings he was making on the gold plates.

The books of Mosiah, Alma, Helaman, Third Nephi, Fourth Nephi, and Mormon are the shortened histories of these people as retold by Mormon. They are mainly written in third person.

Before Mormon died, he gave the records to his son Moroni. Moroni added the history of the Jaredites (the book of Ether), along with his own record, to the writings of his father.

Moroni then sealed up the golden plates of the Book of Mormon and placed them in a sacred place where the Lord watched over and protected them.

In 1823, Moroni appeared as an angel to Joseph Smith in the state of New York. Moroni gave the gold plates to Joseph in 1827 so he could translate the records into our language. The Book of Mormon was written for us and is a testimony of Jesus Christ and His gospel.

A VISUAL EXPLANATION OF THE GOLD PLATES

THE GOLD PLATES	THE BOOKS OF THE BOOK OF MORMON
Mormon's abridgement of the book of Lehi	The 116 manuscript pages lost by Martin Harris
Small plates of Nephi* (written by Nephi and his descendants)	1 Nephi, 2 Nephi, Jacob, Enos, Jarom, Omni
Mormon's writings explaining the insertion of the Small plates of Nephi	Words of Mormon
Mormon's abridgement of the large plates of Nephi**	Mosiah, Alma, Helaman, 3 Nephi, 4 Nephi
Mormon and Moroni's abridgement of the writings of Mormon	Mormon
Moroni's final writings	Moroni
The title page of the Book of Mormon written by Mormon	Title page
Sealed portion—portion of the gold plate that was sealed. Joseph Smith did not translate this part.	(We don't know what was written in this portion.)

*The small plates of Nephi were the plates that Nephi made for him and his descendants to keep sacred writings on. He also included the history of how he and his family left Jerusalem and came to the promised land. Mormon added the small plates of Nephi to his abridged record because the Lord commanded him to. We now know why the Lord wanted this done; He knew that Joseph Smith's translation of the book of Lehi would be lost by Martin Harris. The small plates of Nephi contained some of the same teachings that were written in the book of Lehi.

**The large plates of Nephi were the plates that Nephi made for him and his descendants to keep a history of their people on. Sacred writings were also kept here from the time of King Mosiah.

LEHI'S FAMILY LEAVES JERUSALEM

You can accomplish anything when you have faith in the Lord!

OBJECTIVE

To help children understand the importance of having faith and courage when the Lord asks us to do things that might seem difficult.

BACKGROUND

Lehi and his family are the first people we are introduced to in the Book of Mormon. They lived in Jerusalem around 600 BC (before Christ was born). Lehi was Nephi's father and a prophet of God. Lehi saw a vision and was shown the future destruction of Jerusalem. The people in Jerusalem were angry with Lehi and wanted to kill him.

GOSPEL ART PICTURE KIT

301: Lehi's Family Leaving Jerusalem

WORD QUEST

- yea
- and it came to pass
- stiffneckedness
- murmur
- visionary
- confound
- durst
- stature
- hardness of their hearts
- lowliness of heart
- prosper

VERSES	SUGGESTED QUESTIONS	TREASURES OF KNOWLEDGE
1 Nephi 2:1–4	• Why did the Lord tell Lehi to take his family and leave Jerusalem? (v. 1) • Where did Lehi's family go, and what did they leave behind? (v. 4) • How would you feel if you had to leave your home and belongings and go to a strange place?	**yea:** indeed, truly **and it came to pass:** an ancient phrased used to connect events
1 Nephi 2:5–7	• What are the names of Lehi's wife and children? (v. 5) • What did Lehi do when the family stopped to rest? (v. 7) • Why do you think it is important to express our gratitude?	An offering is a sacrifice, a form of worship that was given to Adam and passed down until the time of Christ. Lehi made sacrifices to show his gratitude to God for delivering him from his enemies and saving his family from the destruction of Jerusalem.
1 Nephi 2:8–11	• What did Lehi want Laman to be like, and why? (v. 9) • What did Lehi want Lemuel to be like, and why? (v. 10) • Why were Laman and Lemuel upset with their father? (v. 11)	**stiffneckedness:** pride; stubbornness **murmur:** complain **visionary:** having visions or dreams
1 Nephi 2:12–15	• Why did Laman and Lemuel murmur? (v. 12) • Did Laman and Lemuel think Jerusalem would be destroyed? (v. 13) • What happened to Laman and Lemuel when Lehi spoke to them? (v. 14)	**confound:** amaze; take aback **durst:** did not dare Lehi's prophecy about Jerusalem came true, and around 610 BC the Babylonians (an empire to the north) destroyed Jerusalem and took many of the Jews captive (see 2 Kings 25).

VERSES	SUGGESTED QUESTIONS	TREASURES OF KNOWLEDGE
1 Nephi 2:16–18	• What did Nephi do when he wanted to know the mysteries of God, and what happened? (v. 16) • How did Sam's reaction to what Nephi told him differ from that of Laman and Lemuel? (vv. 17–18) • Laman and Lemuel murmured because they did not understand God's plan. Nephi, on the other hand, made the effort to pray and ask God to help him believe. What does Nephi's example teach us about what to do when we don't understand something?	**stature:** size **hardness of their hearts:** unwillingness to admit mistakes and change. If someone's heart is hard, they don't want to listen to the teachings of God and His prophets.
1 Nephi 2:19–20, 22	• Why was the Lord pleased with Nephi? (v. 19) • What did the Lord promise Nephi for being obedient? (vv. 20, 22)	**lowliness of heart:** willingness to listen and obey the Lord **prosper:** receive great blessings
1 Nephi 2:21, 23–24	• What did God say would happen if Laman and Lemuel rebelled? • Faith is believing in God and His prophets even when you might not understand all that they are asking you to do. What is something our modern prophet has told us to do that you are doing?	Laman and Lemuel and their descendants did receive a curse upon them (see Alma 3:6–8).

Keeping the commandments can be hard, but the Lord will help you!

THE BRASS PLATES, PART I

OBJECTIVE
To help children learn that the Lord will help them keep His commandments.

BACKGROUND
Lehi and his family were warned by the Lord to leave Jerusalem. They left their home and belongings and traveled far into the wilderness to the Red Sea to escape their enemies and the destruction of Jerusalem (see "Lehi's Journey" in the appendix).

GOSPEL ART PICTURE KIT
Unavailable

WORD QUEST
- forefathers
- hither
- smite
- iniquities

VERSES	SUGGESTED QUESTIONS	TREASURES OF KNOWLEDGE
1 Nephi 3:1–3	• What did the Lord tell Lehi to have his sons go and do? (v. 2) • What did Laban have that Lehi needed? (v. 3) • What was written on the records? (v. 3)	**forefathers:** ancestors (grandparents, great-grandparents, and so forth of a particular person) One of Lehi's forefathers was Joseph who was sold into Egypt by his brothers (1 Nephi 5:14–16).
1 Nephi 3:4–6	• Why did Laman and Lemuel murmur about going back to Jerusalem? (v. 5) • Why would Nephi be "favored of the Lord"? (v. 6)	**hither:** here
1 Nephi 3:7–9	• What was Nephi's reaction to the Lord's commandment? (v. 7) • Does knowing that the Lord will always help you keep His commandments give you the courage to do the right thing? • Laman and Lemuel did what the Lord commanded by returning to Jerusalem; however, they murmured about doing it, while Nephi didn't. How do you think the Lord feels when we complain about keeping the commandments? • What kind of attitude do you have toward keeping the commandments?	
1 Nephi 3:10–12	• How did the brothers choose who would go to Laban's house? (v. 11) • Who was chosen to go? (v. 11)	Casting lots is a way of making a decision, like drawing sticks.

VERSES	SUGGESTED QUESTIONS	TREASURES OF KNOWLEDGE
1 Nephi 3:13–16	• What did Laban say when Laman asked for the plates? (v. 13) • What did the brothers want to do after Laman returned from Laban's house? (v. 14) • What was Nephi's idea for what they should do? (v. 16)	
1 Nephi 3:17–21	• Why was Jerusalem going to be destroyed? (v. 17) • Why was it important for them to get the brass plates? (v. 19–20)	
1 Nephi 3:22–27	• When the brothers offered Laban their gold and silver, what did Laban do? (v. 25) • What happened to their gold and silver? (v. 26) • Where did the brothers hide? (v. 27)	
1 Nephi 3:28–31	• What did Laman and Lemuel do to Nephi and Sam? (v. 28) • What did the angel tell Laman and Lemuel? (v. 29) • After the angel left, what did Laman and Lemuel say? (v. 31)	**smite:** hit **iniquities:** sin or wickedness

We need to obey the Lord, even when we don't understand why.

THE BRASS PLATES, PART II

OBJECTIVE
To help children learn that they need to trust the Lord and do the things He tells them to do, even when they don't understand why.

BACKGROUND
Laban wouldn't give the brass plates to Nephi and his brothers, and he sent his soldiers to kill them. Nephi and his brothers escaped and hid outside of Jerusalem. An angel appeared to the brothers and told them to go back into Jerusalem and get the brass plates.

GOSPEL ART PICTURE KIT
Unavailable

WORD QUEST
- hither and thither
- wroth
- sheath
- hilt
- constrained
- dwindle
- whit
- bade
- diligent
- oath
- lest

VERSES	SUGGESTED QUESTIONS	TREASURES OF KNOWLEDGE
1 Nephi 4:1–3	• What did Nephi say to his brothers? (v. 1) • What example from the scriptures did Nephi use to remind his brothers that the Lord would help them? (v. 2)	**hither and thither:** here and there
1 Nephi 4:4–6	• Which of the brothers went into the city to find Laban? (v. 5) • How did Nephi know where to go and what he was supposed to do? (v. 6) • Do you think Nephi was afraid?	**wroth:** angry
1 Nephi 4:7–13	• What did the Spirit command Nephi to do, and why? (vv. 10–12) • Why was it important for Nephi and his children to have the brass plates? (v. 13)	**sheath:** a case for a sword **hilt:** the handle **constrained:** commanded **dwindle:** gradually diminish
1 Nephi 4:14–17	• What did the Lord promise Nephi? (v. 14) • What was written on the plates of brass? (v. 16) • Why did God deliver Laban to Nephi? (v. 17)	
1 Nephi 4:18–21	• What did Nephi do after Laban had been slain? (vv. 19–20) • Why did Laban's servant think he was talking to Laban? (v. 21)	**whit:** bit

VERSES	SUGGESTED QUESTIONS	TREASURES OF KNOWLEDGE
1 Nephi 4:22–27	• Where did Nephi and Laban's servant go? (v. 24) • Why was he willing to follow Nephi? (v. 26)	**bade:** commanded
1 Nephi 4:28–30	• Why were Nephi's brothers frightened? (v. 28) • How did the servant react when he realized Nephi wasn't with Laban? (v. 30)	
1 Nephi 4:31–35	• Where did Nephi get his strength? (v. 31) • What oath did Nephi make with Laban's servant? (v. 33) • What was Laban's servant's name? (v. 35) • Why did Zoram trust Nephi? (v. 35)	**diligent:** a determination to be obedient **oath:** a promise In Nephi's time, oaths were taken very seriously. A person would rather die than break his oath.
1 Nephi 4:36–38	• Why didn't they want Zoram to return to Jerusalem? (v. 36) • Where did they go after they got the plates? (v. 38)	**lest:** for fear that

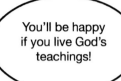

You'll be happy if you live God's teachings!

THE TREE OF LIFE

OBJECTIVE

To help children learn that living the teachings of God will bring them happiness.

BACKGROUND

Lehi was shown a vision about the journey of life and the importance of staying on the right path. Nephi asked God to help him understand his father's dream. He was shown the same vision and told its meaning.

GOSPEL ART PICTURE KIT

Unavailable

Note: "Partake of the Fruit" (on page 136) in the game section is a great way to reinforce the teachings in this lesson.

WORD QUEST

- thereof
- whither
- concourses
- commence

Note: The verses that reference Nephi's interpretations are given in parentheses. They can be read right after reading the verses in Lehi's dream, or you can go back and read them separately.

VERSES	SUGGESTED QUESTIONS	TREASURES OF KNOWLEDGE
1 Nephi 8:9–12 (1 Nephi 11:21–22)	• Describe the fruit that Lehi saw in his dream. (v. 11) • What happened when Lehi partook of the fruit? (v. 12) • What did Lehi want his family to do? (v. 12) • What does the tree represent? (v. 22)	**thereof:** of that
1 Nephi 8:13–18 (1 Nephi 15:26–28)	• Who stood at the head of the river, and who came and partook of the fruit with Lehi? (vv. 14, 16) • Who wouldn't come and partake of the fruit? (vv. 17–18) • What does the water represent? (vv. 27–28)	**whither:** where The fruit represents eternal life. According to Bruce R. McConkie, eternal life is not just life with Heavenly Father, but it is life like His. Eternal life "is the kind, status, type, and quality of life that God himself enjoys."*
1 Nephi 8:19–22 (1 Nephi 11:25)	• Where was the rod of iron located, and where did it lead? (v. 19) • What path did the people get on, and where did it lead? (v. 21) • What does the rod of iron represent, and where does it lead?	**concourses:** crowds **commence:** start The word of God is found in the scriptures, the commandments, and the teachings of the prophets.

* Bruce. R. McConkie, *Mormon Doctrine.* 2d ed. (Salt Lake City: Bookcraft, 1979), 237.

VERSES	SUGGESTED QUESTIONS	TREASURES OF KNOWLEDGE
1 Nephi 8:23–25 (1 Nephi 12:17)	• Why did some people lose their way? (v. 23) • Why did other people not lose their way? (v. 24) • What do the mists of darkness represent? What do they do to us? • What kinds of temptations are you faced with in your life?	Satan will try to tempt us to let go of the iron rod and stop obeying God's commandments. Satan tries to make bad things seem good, and he will try to confuse us and lead us away.
1 Nephi 8:26–28 (1 Nephi 11:35–36)	• What was on the other side of the river? (v. 26) • How did the people in the building treat those who were eating the fruit? (v. 27) • Why do you think the people were ashamed? (v. 28) • Are you ever ashamed of being a member of the Church of Jesus Christ? • What does the great and spacious building represent? (v. 35) • What will eventually happen to the great and spacious building? (v. 36) • What will happen to those who fight against Christ and His Apostles? (v. 36)	The building was lifted off the ground to signify that it had no foundation. That means it was not built on top of something solid and could easily fall. The teachings of the world are not solid and true; they will not help us. We need to build our lives on the teachings of Christ. His way is the right way. He is the only sure foundation.
1 Nephi 8:29–34	• What different places did Lehi see the multitude going to? (vv. 30–33) • Think of your life right now—are you in the great and spacious building of the world, lost in the mists, or holding fast to the iron rod? If you are not where you'd like to be, what changes can you make in your life to get there?	

Following the words of Christ will lead you to eternal life.

THE LIAHONA

OBJECTIVE
To help children learn that faithfully following the words of Christ will lead to eternal life.

BACKGROUND
The Lord told Nephi and his brothers to return to Jerusalem again to get Ishmael's family. Lehi's sons married the daughters of Ishmael, and both families lived in the desert in the Valley of Lemuel. The Lord then told Lehi to pack up their things and begin their journey into the wilderness.

GOSPEL ART PICTURE KIT
302: The Liahona

Note: "Seek and Ye Shall Find" on page 136 in the game section is a fun game to play with this lesson.

WORD QUEST
- curious workmanship
- chastened
- faith
- heed
- slothful

VERSES	SUGGESTED QUESTIONS	TREASURES OF KNOWLEDGE
1 Nephi 16:9–12	• What did Lehi find outside of his tent? (v. 10) • Describe what the ball looked like. (v. 10) • What did it do? (v. 10)	**curious workmanship:** beautifully made
1 Nephi 16:15–17	• What did they do for food while in the wilderness? (v. 15) • What do you think "slaying food by the way" means? • Why couldn't they buy their food from a store or market? • How did the Liahona help them? (v. 16)	
1 Nephi 16:18–20	• Why was everyone so upset? (v. 18) • How might you react if you were in this situation?	
1 Nephi 16:21–25	• How did everyone but Nephi respond to the situation? (v. 22) • What did Nephi ask his father to do? (v. 23) • How did Lehi later feel about his complaining? (v. 25) • What do these verses teach us about how we should respond to difficult challenges?	**chastened:** corrected
1 Nephi 16:26–29	• How did the Liahona work? (v. 28) • What was written on the Liahona? (v. 29)	**faith:** belief and trust in something that is true even when you can't see it (examples: having faith that Heavenly Father and Jesus Christ live; trusting that Heavenly Father knows you and will help you) **heed:** obey

VERSES	SUGGESTED QUESTIONS	TREASURES OF KNOWLEDGE
1 Nephi 16:30–32	• Where did Nephi go? (v. 30) • How did Nephi know where to go and what to do? (v. 30) • How did Nephi's family feel when he returned? (v. 32)	
Alma 37:38–40	• What does the word *Liahona* mean? (v. 38) • Why did Lehi receive the Liahona? (v. 39) • What miracle did they receive? (v. 40)	**slothful:** lazy
Alma 37:41–42	• What happened to the Liahona when Lehi's family didn't have faith? (vv. 41–42)	
Alma 37:43–46	• Alma compares the Liahona to what? (v. 44) • Following the words of Christ will lead us where? (v. 45) • Ask yourself: Am I diligent in following the words of Christ, or am I sometimes lazy and forget to do the things I'm supposed to be doing, like praying, exercising faith, studying the word of God, and keeping the commandments? • What can I do to be better?	" 'These things are not without a shadow' is a way of saying 'These events have symbolic meaning.' "* We receive a type of Liahona when we are baptized and confirmed a member of the Church. It is the Holy Ghost. The Holy Ghost will guide and direct us in our lives. But if we are not righteous, the Holy Ghost, like the Liahona, cannot be with us to help us.

* Joseph Fielding McConkie and Robert L. Millet, *Doctrinal Commentary on the Book of Mormon, Vol. 3* (Salt Lake City: Bookcraft, 1991), 282.

You can accomplish anything the Lord asks you to do.

NEPHI BUILDS A SHIP

OBJECTIVE

To help children learn that they can accomplish anything the Lord asks them to do.

BACKGROUND

Lehi and his family traveled in the wilderness for eight years before they arrived at the land of Bountiful, a beautiful place by the sea, with plenty of food.

GOSPEL ART PICTURE KIT

303: Nephi Subdues His Rebellious Brothers

WORD QUEST
- wade
- sojourn
- ore
- molten
- bellows
- swift to do iniquity
- rent with anguish
- wrought

VERSES	SUGGESTED QUESTIONS	TREASURES OF KNOWLEDGE
1 Nephi 17:1–5	• What was traveling in the wilderness like for Lehi's family? (vv. 1–2) • What does Nephi tell us God will do for the children of men if they keep the commandments? (v. 3) • How does that make you feel? • How long did they travel in the wilderness? (v. 4) • Why did they call the land Bountiful? (v. 5)	**wade:** to get through with effort and difficulty **sojourn:** travel
1 Nephi 17:6–8	• Where did the Lord tell Nephi to go? (v. 7) • What did the Lord tell Nephi to do? (v. 8) • Nephi had never built a ship. How might you feel if the Lord asked you to do something like that?	
1 Nephi 17:9–11, 16	• What did Nephi ask the Lord to help him to do? (v. 9) • Describe how Nephi made the tools. (vv. 11, 16)	**ore:** metal from a mineral **molten:** melted; able to be molded **bellows:** an instrument used for blowing fires
1 Nephi 17:17–18	• How did Laman and Lemuel react when Nephi told them he was building a ship? (vv. 17–18)	
1 Nephi 17:19–21	• How did Nephi feel about Laman and Lemuel's reaction? (v. 19) • What were Laman and Lemuel so angry about? (vv. 20–21)	
1 Nephi 17:23, 44	• In what way were Laman and Lemuel like the Jews? (v. 44)	

VERSES	SUGGESTED QUESTIONS	TREASURES OF KNOWLEDGE
1 Nephi 17:45–47	• Why couldn't Laman and Lemuel feel the Holy Ghost? (v. 45) • Why was Nephi's soul "rent with anguish"? (v. 47) • Laman and Lemuel had seen an angel and the power of God work miracles, yet when life became difficult they began to complain and doubt. Do you ever find yourself complaining when life is hard? What can you do to be more like Nephi and less like Laman and Lemuel?	**swift to do iniquity:** quick to sin **rent with anguish:** filled with pain
1 Nephi 17:48–51	• When Laman and Lemuel became angry with Nephi, what did they want to do to him? (v. 48) • What did Nephi say to Laman and Lemuel when they tried to take him? (vv. 48–49) • What did Nephi say he could do if God commanded him? (v. 50) • What can God help you accomplish in your life if you have enough faith?	**wrought:** influenced
1 Nephi 17:52–55	• Why were Laman and Lemuel afraid to touch Nephi? (v. 52) • What did the Lord tell Nephi to do and why? (v. 53) • What happened to Laman and Lemuel when Nephi "stretched forth his hand"? (v. 54) • What did Laman and Lemuel say and do after Nephi shocked them? (v. 55) • Who did Nephi tell Laman and Lemuel to worship? (v. 55)	

The Lord will guide and direct you if you pray and ask for help.

TRAVELING TO THE PROMISED LAND

OBJECTIVE
To help children learn that the Lord will guide and direct them in their lives if they will pray and ask for help.

BACKGROUND
While Lehi and his family were in the land of Bountiful, the Lord commanded Nephi to build a ship to take the family to the promised land.

GOSPEL ART PICTURE KIT
304: Lehi and His People Arrive in the Promised Land

WORD QUEST
- timbers
- humble
- soberness
- tempest
- sore

VERSES	SUGGESTED QUESTIONS	TREASURES OF KNOWLEDGE
1 Nephi 18:1–4	• What do you think Nephi means when he says the ship was not built "after the manner of men"? (v. 2) • What did Nephi often go and do so he would know how to build the ship? (v. 3) • What should we do when we need help with something in our lives?	**timbers:** wood used for building the ship **humble:** trusting in and following the will of God
1 Nephi 18:5–8	• What did the family take with them on the ship? (v. 6) • What were the names of Lehi's sons who were born in the wilderness? (v. 7)	
1 Nephi 18:9–11	• What were Laman and Lemuel and some of the others doing that was wrong? (v. 9) • Why were Laman and Lemuel angry with Nephi, and what did they do to him? (vv. 10–11) • Why did the Lord allow them to tie Nephi up? (v. 11)	**soberness:** self-control
1 Nephi 18:12–14	• When did the Liahona stop working? (v. 12) • What happened after the Liahona stopped working? (v. 13)	**tempest:** violent storm **sore:** great

VERSES	SUGGESTED QUESTIONS	TREASURES OF KNOWLEDGE
1 Nephi 18:15–16	• What caused Laman and Lemuel to finally untie Nephi? (v. 15) • What did Nephi do after they let him go? (v. 16)	
1 Nephi 18:17–19	• What did Laman and Lemuel say to Lehi when he tried to help Nephi, and how did it affect Lehi and Sariah? (vv. 17–18) • How was the rest of Nephi's family affected by Laman and Lemuel's cruelty? (v. 19)	
1 Nephi 18:20–22	• What was the only thing that softened Laman and Lemuel's hearts? (v. 20) • What made the Liahona start working again? (v. 21)	
1 Nephi 18:23–25	• What did Lehi's family do when they arrived in the promised land? (v. 24) • What did they find there? (v. 25)	

In this lesson and previous lessons, we have read about many of Nephi's experiences. Nephi was a man of great faith. Ask each person in the family to give one of their favorite examples of Nephi demonstrating faith in the Lord. Are there experiences in your life where you have shown the same great faith?

For younger children:
Have the children draw a picture of their favorite story of Nephi. Ask them why they chose this story and what they can do to be more like Nephi.

When you serve others, you also serve God.

KING BENJAMIN'S TEACHINGS ON SERVICE

OBJECTIVE
To help children learn that when they serve others they are serving God.

BACKGROUND
King Benjamin was a righteous Nephite who lived in the land of Zarahemla. (See "Chart of Nephite Leaders" and "Book of Mormon Cities" in the appendix.) He was a good king who served his people faithfully. Before he died, he asked his son Mosiah to gather all of the people in the land to hear his last words.

GOSPEL ART PICTURE KIT
307: King Benjamin Addresses His People

WORD QUEST
- waxed
- suffered
- boast
- unprofitable servant
- indebted
- transgress
- succor
- vain
- repent
- condemn
- wo
- covet
- remission
- sin

Note to parents: For this lesson you can have the family make tents out of blankets and chairs. Have everyone but one family member sit in their tent doors as they listen to someone dressed up like King Benjamin reading the verses (except vv. 1–8) from this lesson while standing on a chair.

VERSES	SUGGESTED QUESTIONS	TREASURES OF KNOWLEDGE
Mosiah 2:1–2	• Where did the people gather to hear King Benjamin speak? (v. 1) • Why were they unable to number the people who came to hear King Benjamin? (v. 2)	**waxed:** increased
Mosiah 2:5–8	• What did the families do when they arrived at the temple? (vv. 5–6) • Why did King Benjamin build a tower to speak to the people? (v. 7) • How did the people who were too far away to hear his voice learn what he had taught? (v. 8)	
Mosiah 2:9, 12	• Why did King Benjamin want the people to open their ears? Their hearts? Their minds? (v. 9) • Did King Benjamin receive gold and silver from the people because he was their king? (v. 12)	**suffered:** allowed **boast:** brag
Mosiah 2:16–18	• When you serve others, who are you also serving? (v. 17) • How do you think you are serving God when you serve others?	

VERSES	SUGGESTED QUESTIONS	TREASURES OF KNOWLEDGE
Mosiah 2:19–21	• What are some of the things King Benjamin is reminding his people that God does for them? (vv. 20–21)	**unprofitable servant:** one who is unable to pay God back for all He's done
Mosiah 2:22–24	• What does God require of us? (v. 22) • What will God do for us if we keep His commandments? (v. 22) • What are we indebted to God for? (v. 23)	**indebted:** owing someone something
Mosiah 4:14–15	• Who are you serving when you fight and argue? (v. 14) • The devil is an enemy to what? (v. 14) • What should parents teach their children? (v. 15) • How should children act towards one another?	**transgress:** to break the law
Mosiah 4:16–18	• Who should we help? (v. 16) • Do you think it is right to judge others who need help? (v. 17) • What will happen if we judge others and don't repent? (v. 18)	**succor:** help **vain:** without success **repent:** to change When we repent, we feel bad for the things we've done wrong, and we stop doing them.
Mosiah 4:19, 21	• Who do we depend on for all our needs? (vv. 19, 21) • What does God give to us? (v. 21) • Why should we give to those who are in need? (v. 21)	

VERSES	SUGGESTED QUESTIONS	TREASURES OF KNOWLEDGE
Mosiah 4:22–23	• Who does our life belong to? (v. 22) • How does God feel if we don't share with others?	**condemn:** to judge **wo:** exclamation of sorrow
Mosiah 4:24–26	• If we are unable to give, what should we say in our hearts? (v. 24) • What are some ways we can help others? (v. 26) • Do you feel that you give freely to others when you are able to? • In your thoughts and heart do you judge those who are in need?	**covet:** to desire something Coveting is wrong when we want the things of the world more than the things of God. **remission:** forgiveness **sin:** to knowingly break a law Elder Orson F. Whitney stated that "a man sins when he does the opposite of what he knows to be right. One cannot commit sin unless he knows better than to do the thing in which the sin consists."*

* Bruce R. McConkie, *Mormon Doctrine*. 2d ed. (Salt Lake City: Bookcraft, 1979), 735.

You should always stand up for what you know is right, even if it's hard.

ABINADI'S COURAGE

OBJECTIVE
To help children learn to always stand up for their beliefs and what they know is right, no matter what the consequences are.

BACKGROUND
A prophet named Abinadi went to the land of Lehi-Nephi to preach repentance to King Noah and his followers. King Noah was Zeniff's son. He was a wicked man who did not keep God's commandments. (See "Book of Mormon Cities" in the appendix for an explanation of the inhabitants of the land of Lehi-Nephi.)

GOSPEL ART PICTURE KIT
308: Abinadi before King Noah

WORD QUEST
- abominations
- whoredoms
- prophesy
- bondage
- descendant
- scourged
- faggots

VERSES	SUGGESTED QUESTIONS	TREASURES OF KNOWLEDGE
Mosiah 11:20–21	• What did Abinadi prophesy to the people? (v. 20) • What did God say he would do to the people if they would not repent? (v. 21)	**abominations:** wrongdoings **whoredoms:** immoral acts **prophesy:** to speak the will of God **bondage:** having your freedom taken away
Mosiah 11:26–29	• What happened when the people tried to take Abinadi? (v. 26) • Why did King Noah want to kill Abinadi? (v. 28) • Why didn't the people listen to Abinadi and repent? (v. 29)	The phrases "blinded" and "hard heart" refer to an unwillingness to see and feel right from wrong. It is a choice to not listen to God and to not obey His commandments.
Mosiah 12:1, 9	• How much time passed before Abinadi came back, and why didn't the people recognize him? (v. 1) • What did the people do to Abinadi? (v. 9)	
Mosiah 12:13–16	• Did the people think they were doing anything wrong? (v. 14) • Who did they seem to have more trust in, God or the king? (v. 15)	
Mosiah 12:17–19	• What did King Noah do to Abinadi? (v. 17) • Why did the priests want to ask Abinadi questions? (v. 19) • How did Abinadi answer the priests? (v. 19)	

VERSES	SUGGESTED QUESTIONS	TREASURES OF KNOWLEDGE
Mosiah 13:1–5	• What did Abinadi say when King Noah and his priests tried to take him? (v. 3) • Why was God protecting Abinadi? (v. 3) • What happened to Abinadi's face when he was talking? (v. 5)	
Mosiah 13:6–10	• How did Abinadi's teachings affect the people? (vv. 7–8) • What did Abinadi say would happen? (v. 10) (Note: The remaining verses in chapter 13 are Abinadi's teachings of the Ten Commandments. These verses will be studied in the next lesson.)	Abinadi is warning the king that whatever the king does to Abinadi will later happen to the king (see Mosiah 19:20).
Mosiah 17:1–4	• Who was Alma a descendant of? (v. 2) • What did King Noah do to Alma? (v. 3) • What did Alma do while he was hiding from the king? (v. 4)	**descendant:** a child, grandchild, or great-grandchild of a particular person
Mosiah 17:5–10	• What accusation did they have against Abinadi? (v. 8) • What would have happened to Abinadi if he had denied his teachings? (v. 8) • Why wouldn't Abinadi deny his teachings? (vv. 9–10)	The real reason King Noah put Abinadi to death "is shown in [his] statement that he would spare Abinadi if he would recall [his words]. One of the methods of the guilty is to destroy those who have exposed their guilt. Abinadi's words condemned Noah for [his] sinful ways, so Noah sought the life of Abinadi."*

* *Book of Mormon Student Manual.* (Salt Lake City: The Church of Jesus Christ of Latter-day Saints, 1982), 64.

VERSES	SUGGESTED QUESTIONS	TREASURES OF KNOWLEDGE
Mosiah 17:11–13	• Why didn't the king release Abinadi even though he was afraid? (v. 12) • What did the people do to Abinadi? (v. 13)	**scourged:** whipped **faggots:** a bundle of sticks
Mosiah 17:14–18	• Name five things that Abinadi prophesied would happen to the people.	Abinadi's prophecies about what would happen in the future came true (Mosiah 19:20; Alma 25:11–12).
Mosiah 17:19–20	• What does God do to those who "destroy his people"? (v. 19) • What prophet in the latter-days also "sealed the truth of his words by his death"?	

What are some ways that you keep the commandments?

THE COMMANDMENTS

OBJECTIVE

To help children gain a better understanding of what the commandments are and how they can keep them.

BACKGROUND

Abinadi preached the importance of keeping the Ten Commandments to King Noah and his followers. When Jesus Christ visited the Nephites, he taught them to love others and to be like him.

GOSPEL ART PICTURE KIT

Unavailable

WORD QUEST

- graven images
- guiltless
- hallowed
- broken heart
- contrite spirit
- despitefully use
- mete

VERSES	SUGGESTED QUESTIONS	TREASURES OF KNOWLEDGE
Mosiah 12:35–36	• What is the commandment that Abinadi gives in these verses? • Are there "graven images" in your life that keep you from worshipping God with all your heart?	**graven images:** material objects that are worshipped or loved more than Heavenly Father
Mosiah 13:15	• What is the commandment given in this verse? • How should we speak the Lord's name?	**guiltless:** innocent Saying God's name in vain is saying it in an irreverent or disrespectful way.
Mosiah 13:16–19	• How are we supposed to spend the Sabbath day? (v. 18) • Are there ways you can better keep this commandment in your home?	**hallowed:** holy
Mosiah 13:20	• What is the commandment given in this verse? • How should we treat our parents?	"Honoring your parents" means appreciating, showing respect for, and obeying them.
Mosiah 13:21–24	• What five commandments are given in these verses? • Who are our neighbors? • Why do you think it's wrong to covet?	To "bear false witness" means to lie, be dishonest, or say untrue things about someone. (See page 25 for an explanation of "covet.")

VERSES	SUGGESTED QUESTIONS	TREASURES OF KNOWLEDGE
3 Nephi 11:38	• What does Christ tell us we must do? • Why do we need to be baptized?	See Mosiah 3:19 for an explanation of becoming as a little child.
3 Nephi 12:19–20	• Name four commandments Christ gives in verse 19. • What do we need to do to enter into the kingdom of heaven? (v. 20)	**broken heart:** feeling bad for the things you have done wrong **contrite spirit:** having a desire to change and repent
3 Nephi 12:43–44	• How should we treat our enemies? (v. 44) • Why do you think Christ wants us to pray for our enemies?	**despitefully use:** hate or hurt
3 Nephi 14:1–2	• Why do you think it's wrong to judge others? • How will we be judged?	**mete:** measure (You will be judged by God the same way you judge others.)

Have each member of the family list as many of the commandments as they can remember. Challenge each person to pick one or two of the commandments that they need to work on keeping better. Ask each person to set a goal to learn more about that commandment and why Heavenly Father has given it to us, and to try harder to keep that commandment.

When you're baptized, you make covenants with Heavenly Father.

ALMA BAPTIZES

OBJECTIVE

To help children learn that when they are baptized, they make promises to Heavenly Father, and if they keep them He promises to bless and help them.

BACKGROUND

Alma was one of King Noah's priests, and he believed the teachings of Abinadi. This made the king angry and he sent his guards to kill Alma. But Alma was able to hide from the king, and while he was hiding he wrote down the teachings of Abinadi.

GOSPEL ART PICTURE KIT

309: Alma Baptizes in the Waters of Mormon

WORD QUEST

- resurrection
- redemption
- resorted thither
- burden
- mourn
- covenant
- authority
- ordained
- apprised

VERSES	SUGGESTED QUESTIONS	TREASURES OF KNOWLEDGE
Mosiah 18:1–3	• Who was Alma hiding from? (v. 1) • Why did Alma have to teach in private? (v. 3)	**resurrection:** the reuniting of body and spirit forever **redemption:** saving from the consequences of sin Through the Atonement, Jesus Christ became our Redeemer. If it wasn't for Jesus' Atonement, we wouldn't be able to live with Heavenly Father again because of our sins and weaknesses. Jesus paid the price for our sins and has the power to save us from their consequences.
Mosiah 18:4–7	• Where did Alma hide from the king? (vv. 4–5) • What did the people who believed Alma's teachings do? (vv. 6–7) • What did Alma teach the people? (v. 7)	**resorted thither:** went there The waters of Mormon were in the borders of the land of Nephi. The prophet Mormon was named after this place (Alma 5:3; 3 Nephi 5:12).
Mosiah 18:8–10	• Name and discuss the four things Alma told the people they needed to be willing to do if they were baptized. (vv. 8–9) • What does Alma say their part of the covenant is? (v. 10) • What did Alma say the Lord would do if they kept their covenants? (v. 10)	**burden:** something that is difficult to deal with **mourn:** to feel sorrow **covenant:** a two-way promise between us and God

VERSES	SUGGESTED QUESTIONS	TREASURES OF KNOWLEDGE
Mosiah 18:8–10 (continued)	• If you have been baptized, you made the same covenants. How are you doing at keeping them?	God will never break a covenant. He will always do what He has promised as long as we do our part.
Mosiah 18:11–13	• How did the people respond to what Alma had taught them? (v. 11) • Who was the first person to be baptized? (v. 12) • Where did Alma receive the authority to baptize? (v. 13)	**authority:** the right to exercise the power of the priesthood
Mosiah 18:14–15	• What did Alma do when he baptized Helam? (v. 14) • How did Alma and Helam feel after being baptized? (v. 14)	
Mosiah 18:16–17	• How many people were baptized? (v. 16) • Whose church did the people belong to? (v. 17) • Whose church do you belong to if you've been baptized?	
Mosiah 18:18–20	• By whose authority did Alma ordain priests? (v. 18) • What did Alma tell the priests to teach to the people? (vv. 19–20)	**ordained:** given the priesthood

VERSES	SUGGESTED QUESTIONS	TREASURES OF KNOWLEDGE
Mosiah 18:21–23	• How did Alma want the people to treat each other? (v. 21) • What commandments did Alma give to the people? (vv. 23–24) • Are these things we should be doing also?	"Hearts knit together in unity" means that the people would love and care for one another equally.
Mosiah 18:24–26	• How often did the people gather together, and what did they do? (v. 25) • What did the priests receive for their labors? (v. 26)	
Mosiah 18:27–29	• What did Alma teach the people about giving? (vv. 27–28) • How should they "impart of their substance?" (v. 28) • Did the people obey this commandment? (v. 29)	To "impart of your substance" means to give some of your possessions (food, clothes, money, etc.) to others in need.
Mosiah 18:31–35	• Why did King Noah send his armies after Alma and his followers? (v. 33) • What did Alma and the people do when they found out the king had discovered them? (v. 34) • How many people were there? (v. 35)	**apprised:** informed

THE PEOPLE OF LIMHI ESCAPE FROM BONDAGE

God will always help you get through the hard times.

OBJECTIVE
To help children learn that God will help them find ways to overcome their burdens.

BACKGROUND
Limhi was king of the Nephites living in the land of Lehi-Nephi after his father, King Noah was burned to death by his people. During this same time, King Mosiah II (son of King Benjamin) was the king of the Nephites living in Zarahemla.

GOSPEL ART PICTURE KIT
Unavailable

WORD QUEST
- teasings
- endeavor
- boldness
- grievous to be borne
- tribute
- hitherto
- hearkened
- proclamation
- subjects

VERSES	SUGGESTED QUESTIONS	TREASURES OF KNOWLEDGE
Mosiah 7:1–4	• Why did King Mosiah send a group of men to the land of Lehi-Nephi? (v. 1) • Who was the leader of the group of men? (v. 3) • Who was Ammon a descendant of? (v. 3) • How long was the group lost in the wilderness? (v. 4)	**teasings:** continual questions/requests Review with the family who Ammon and Zarahemla are by looking them up in the "Who's Who" section in the appendix. The terms "up" and "down" refer to elevation, not direction.*
Mosiah 7:5–8	• What happened to Ammon and his brethren when they met the king? (v. 7) • How long were they in prison? (v. 8)	
Mosiah 7:9–11	• What was the name of the king in the land of Lehi-Nephi? (v. 9) • Who were the king's father and grandfather? (v. 9) • Why did Limhi allow Ammon and his brethren to live instead of killing them? (v. 11)	
Mosiah 7:12–13	• What did Ammon say to the king when he was allowed to speak? (vv. 12–13)	**endeavor:** attempt **boldness:** courage
Mosiah 7:14–16	• Why was Limhi happy about what Ammon had told him? (v. 14–15) • What did King Limhi have his guards do for Ammon and his brethren? (v. 16)	**grievous to be borne:** hard to endure **tribute:** money or valuables that one king pays to another in return for peace

* John L. Sorenson, *Mormon's Map.* (Provo, Utah: FARMS, 2000).

VERSES	SUGGESTED QUESTIONS	TREASURES OF KNOWLEDGE
Mosiah 22:1–2	• Why didn't the people of Limhi want to fight against the Lamanites to gain their freedom? (v. 2)	
Mosiah 22:3–8	• What was Gideon's plan for how they could escape? (vv. 6–8)	**hitherto:** until this time **hearkened:** listened and paid attention **proclamation:** an announcement
Mosiah 22:9–11	• Did King Limhi and the people do what Gideon had planned? • How were they able to get past the Lamanite guards? (v. 10)	
Mosiah 22:12–14	• What did the people take with them when they left? (v. 12) • Where did Limhi and his people finally arrive after traveling for many days? (v. 13)	**subjects:** people under the rule of a king The records found by the people of Limhi were the records of the Jaredites. (Mosiah 8: 6–12)
Mosiah 22:15–16	• What did the Lamanites do when they discovered King Limhi and his people were gone? (v. 15) • Why do you think the Lamanites were unable to find King Limhi and his people?	

Everyone has trials, even the righteous. But God will help us get through them.

ALMA'S PEOPLE ARE PUT IN BONDAGE

OBJECTIVE

To help children learn that even righteous people have trials; to help them trust in God's plan for them.

WORD QUEST
- exhorted
- chasten

BACKGROUND

Alma, who was once a priest of King Noah, believed the words of the prophet Abinadi and baptized many people at the Waters of Mormon. King Noah was angry with Alma and sent his army to kill Alma and all of his followers.

GOSPEL ART PICTURE KIT

Unavailable

VERSES	SUGGESTED QUESTIONS	TREASURES OF KNOWLEDGE
Mosiah 23:1–5	• How did Alma know the armies of King Noah were coming? (v. 1) • How long did they travel in the wilderness? (v. 3) • Describe the place that Alma and his followers found. (v. 4) • What did they do when they arrived there? (v. 5)	
Mosiah 23:19–20, 25–26	• What was the name of their city? (v. 19) • Who did the people see outside of the city? (v. 25) • Why were they afraid? (v. 26)	
Mosiah 23:27–29	• What was Alma's counsel to his people? (v. 27) • What did the people ask the Lord to do? (v. 28) • What did the Lamanites do? (v. 29)	**exhorted:** strongly urged
Mosiah 23:30–32	• Who had the Lamanite army been chasing? (v. 30) • Who did the Lamanite army find? (v. 31) • Who was Amulon? (v. 32)	The wicked priests of King Noah escaped into the wilderness when the Lamanites attacked the city of Lehi-Nephi. They kidnapped Lamanite women and forced them to be their wives (see Mosiah 19–20).
Mosiah 23:33–35	• Why didn't the Lamanites destroy the priests? (vv. 33–34) • What were the Lamanites searching for when they found the city of Helam? (v. 35)	The Lamanites lived in the land of Nephi. Even though it was named after Nephi, the Nephites had left it long ago. (See "Nephite Cities and Occupants" in the appendix.)

VERSES	SUGGESTED QUESTIONS	TREASURES OF KNOWLEDGE
Mosiah 23:36–39	• What promise did the Lamanites make with Alma? Did they keep their promise? (vv. 36–37) • What did the Lamanites do to Alma's people? (v. 37) • Who did the Lamanites appoint to be a ruler over Alma's people? (v. 39) • Alma and his people were good and righteous. Why do you think the Lord allowed them to be put into bondage by the Lamanites? (vv. 21–24)	
Mosiah 23:21–24	• According to Mormon, why does the Lord "chasten His people"? (v. 21) • What will happen to those who put their trust in God? (v. 22) • What do you think eventually happened to Alma's people? (v. 24)	**chasten:** to punish or subject to trials Sometimes the Lord allows difficult things to happen to us to give us the chance to change and grow; He loves us and wants us to become better people. To be "lifted up at the last day" means to be resurrected and receive eternal life. Jesus Christ is "the God of Abraham and Isaac and of Jacob."

ALMA'S PEOPLE ARE DELIVERED FROM THE LAMANITES

> You can get through difficult times if you have faith and patience.

OBJECTIVE
To help children learn that faith and patience will strengthen them through difficult times.

BACKGROUND
Alma and the people in the land of Helam were discovered by the Lamanites who were lost in the wilderness after looking for Limhi and his people. The Lamanites put Alma and his people into bondage. The Lamanite king appointed Amulon to rule over them. (Amulon was the leader of the wicked priests of King Noah.)

GOSPEL ART PICTURE KIT
Unavailable

WORD QUEST
- favor
- cunning
- plunder
- persecute
- hereafter
- affliction
- haste

VERSES	SUGGESTED QUESTIONS	TREASURES OF KNOWLEDGE
Mosiah 24:1, 4	• What did the Lamanite king appoint Amulon and his brethren to do for the Lamanites?	**favor:** support
Mosiah 24:5–7	• What did Amulon not teach the Lamanites about? (v. 5) • What were the Lamanite people like? (vv. 5–7)	**cunning:** deceptive, not honest **plunder:** to rob or steal
Mosiah 24:8–9	• How did Amulon treat Alma's people? (v. 8) • Why was Amulon angry with Alma? (v. 9)	**persecute:** to cause suffering
Mosiah 24:10–12	• What would happen to Alma's people if they prayed? (v. 11) • How did the people talk to the Lord if they couldn't pray? (v. 12) • How does that make you feel to know that God knows the thoughts of your heart?	
Mosiah 24:13–15	• What did the Lord say He would do for Alma and his people? (v. 13) • How did the Lord help them with their burdens? (v. 14) • How did the people respond to the "will of the Lord"? (v. 15)	**hereafter:** from this time **affliction:** something that is hard to bear
Mosiah 24:16–19	• Why did the Lord deliver Alma's people from bondage? (v. 16) • How did the Lord deliver them from bondage? (vv. 18–19)	

VERSES	SUGGESTED QUESTIONS	TREASURES OF KNOWLEDGE
Mosiah 24:20–22	• Why did they call the valley Alma? (v. 20) • What did the people do when they stopped to rest? (vv. 21–22) • Why do you think it's important to give thanks to God?	
Mosiah 24:23–25	• Why did Alma and his people have to leave the valley? (v. 23) • How long did the people journey in the wilderness? (v. 25) • Where did they finally arrive? (v. 25) • How was Alma's escape from the Lamanites different from Limhi's? (Mosiah 22:9–13)	**haste:** hurry

THE JOURNEY OF ALMA AND HIS PEOPLE

1. LEHI-NEPHI
Under the rule of King Noah, Abinadi preached here.

2. WATERS OF MORMON
Alma baptized many people who joined the Church.

4. ZARAHEMLA
Alma and his people were delivered from the Lamanites by the Lord and fled to the land of Zarahemla, where they lived with King Mosiah and the Nephites.

3. HELAM
The people escaped from King Noah and prospered in this city until they were discovered and put in bondage by the Lamanites.

45

Sin causes unhappiness. Living righteously will bring you joy.

ALMA THE YOUNGER

OBJECTIVE
To help children learn that sin causes suffering and unhappiness. Living righteously and spreading the gospel brings joy.

BACKGROUND
Alma the Younger was the son of Alma the Elder (who we read about in the previous lessons). Alma the Elder was a righteous man; but his son Alma the Younger and the sons of King Mosiah were rebellious and did not keep the commandments. This caused Alma the Elder and King Mosiah to be very sad, and they prayed that the Lord would help their sons.

GOSPEL ART PICTURE KIT
321: Conversion of Alma the Younger

WORD QUEST
- idolatrous
- flattery
- racked
- harrowed up
- exquisite
- ceasing

VERSES	SUGGESTED QUESTIONS	TREASURES OF KNOWLEDGE
Mosiah 27:8–10	• What kind of life was Alma living? (v. 8) • How did Alma's words and actions affect the people? (v. 9) • What did Alma and the sons of Mosiah do secretly? (v. 10)	**idolatrous:** worshipping false gods **flattery:** false praise
Mosiah 27:11–14	• Who appeared to Alma and the sons of King Mosiah? (v. 11) • How did the angel appear, and what did his voice sound like? (v. 11) • What happened when the angel spoke? (v. 12) • What did the angel say to Alma? (v. 13) • Why do you think God sent an angel to Alma? (v. 14)	
Mosiah 27:15–17	• What was the angel's message to Alma? (v. 16) • What did the angel tell Alma to remember? (v. 16) (Note: The following verses are from Alma's own account of what happened to him.)	
Alma 36:10–11	• What happened to Alma after the angel left? (v. 10) • Why was Alma afraid? (v. 11)	
Alma 36:12–16	• What was causing Alma so much suffering? (v. 13) • Why didn't Alma want to be in the presence of God? (v. 14) • How long did Alma suffer? (v. 16) • How do you feel when you do something wrong?	**racked:** filled with pain **harrowed up:** in great distress

VERSES	SUGGESTED QUESTIONS	TREASURES OF KNOWLEDGE
Alma 36:17–19	• What did Alma remember that his father had taught? (v. 17) • Who did Alma cry out to for help, and what happened when he did? (vv. 18–19)	
Alma 36:20–23	• What was Alma's soul filled with? (v. 20) • What did Alma see? (v. 22) • How did Alma feel now about being in the presence of God? (v. 22) • What did Alma say and do when he awakened? (v. 23)	**exquisite:** intense To be born of God means to have a change of heart, and a desire to do good things.
Alma 36:24–26	• What did Alma spend his time doing after he repented? (v. 24) • How did Alma feel when he taught others about God? (v. 25) • Have you shared the gospel with others? If so, how did it make you feel? If not, how do you think you and those you could share it with would feel if you did?	**ceasing:** stopping

AMMON— MISSIONARY TO THE LAMANITES

> You need to be a good friend and example in order to share the gospel.

OBJECTIVE

To help children learn that they need to be good examples and friends to those people they wish to share the gospel with.

WORD QUEST

- swollen
- contend
- slew

BACKGROUND

Ammon was one of the sons of King Mosiah. He was with Alma the Younger when the angel appeared, and he was also converted to the gospel. Ammon and each of his brothers turned down their father's request to become the new king and rule over the land of Zarahemla. Instead they went to preach the gospel to the Lamanites, their enemies. God promised King Mosiah that none of his sons would be killed on their missions to the Lamanites.

GOSPEL ART PICTURE KIT

310: Ammon Defends the Flocks of King Lamoni

VERSES	SUGGESTED QUESTIONS	TREASURES OF KNOWLEDGE
Alma 17:19–21	• Who was the land of Ishmael named after? (v. 19) • What happened to Ammon when he entered the land of Ishmael? (v. 20) • What was the name of the king, and who was he a descendant of? (v. 21)	Review with the family who Ishmael was, by looking him up in the "Who's Who" in the appendix.
Alma 17:22–25	• What did King Lamoni offer to Ammon? (v. 24) • What kind of servant was Ammon? (v. 25) • Why do you think Ammon wanted to be the king's servant?	
Alma 17:26–28	• What did the other Lamanites do to the king's flocks? (v. 27) • Why were the king's servants afraid? (v. 28)	
Alma 17:29–30	• Why did Ammon want to show the servants that he had the power of God with him? (v. 29)	**swollen:** filled
Alma 17:31–34	• What did Ammon ask the king's servants to do with the flocks? (vv. 31, 33) • Did Ammon take any of the servants with him to fight? (v. 33) • Why do you think Ammon was not afraid to fight alone against these men?	**contend:** to fight

VERSES	SUGGESTED QUESTIONS	TREASURES OF KNOWLEDGE
Alma 17:35–36	• Why did the men not fear Ammon? (v. 35) • What did Ammon do to the men who were trying to scatter the flocks? (v. 36) • What did the Lamanites do when they couldn't kill Ammon with their stones? (v. 36)	**slew:** killed
Alma 17:37–39	• What did Ammon do when the men tried to kill him? (v. 37) • After the Lamanites ran away, what did Ammon and the servants do with the arms? (v. 39) • How do you think this experience helped Ammon to be a good missionary?	

Be sure to listen to the Spirit when you teach others about the gospel.

AMMON TEACHES KING LAMONI

OBJECTIVE
To help children learn the importance of listening to the Spirit when teaching others about the gospel.

BACKGROUND
Ammon went on a mission to the Lamanites in the land of Ishmael. He became a servant to King Lamoni. Ammon saved the king's flocks and cut off the arms of the men who tried to kill him.

GOSPEL ART PICTURE KIT
Unavailable

WORD QUEST
- countenance
- notwithstanding
- guile
- expound
- mercy

VERSES	SUGGESTED QUESTIONS	TREASURES OF KNOWLEDGE
Alma 18:1–3	• Who did King Lamoni think Ammon was? (v. 2) • What did the servants say to the king? (v. 3)	
Alma 18:4–7	• Why did the king think the Great Spirit had come? (v. 4) • Where did King Lamoni learn about the Great Spirit? (v. 5) • Why had King Lamoni killed so many of his servants? (v. 6)	
Alma 18:8–11	• Where was Ammon, and what was he doing? (v. 9) • Why was the king impressed with Ammon? (v. 10)	
Alma 18:12–15	• Why did Ammon want to leave the presence of the king? (v. 12) • What did the servant call Ammon and why? (v. 13) • How long did the king wait to answer Ammon's question and why did he wait so long? (v. 14)	**countenance:** an expression of the face
Alma 18:16–19	• How did Ammon know what the king was thinking? (v. 16) • Why did the king marvel? (v. 18) • What did the king ask Ammon, and what was Ammon's reply? (vv. 18–19)	**notwithstanding:** nevertheless

VERSES	SUGGESTED QUESTIONS	TREASURES OF KNOWLEDGE
Alma 18:20–23	• King Lamoni told Ammon he would give him anything if Ammon would do what? (v. 21) • What did Ammon say he wanted from the king? (v. 22)	**guile:** part of a plan—this is what Ammon wanted to happen
Alma 18:24–29	• What did King Lamoni believe in? (vv. 26–27) • What did the king not know about? (v. 29)	
Alma 18:30–32	• Where is heaven? (v. 30) • What does God know about each of us? (v. 32)	
Alma 18:33–35	• In whose image are we created? (v. 34) • Where did Ammon receive his knowledge and power from? (v. 35)	To be created in God's image means we look like Him; we have a body like He does.
Alma 18:36–39	• Name five things that Ammon taught to King Lamoni and his servants.	**expound:** to further explain or clarify
Alma 18:40–43	• What was King Lamoni's reaction to Ammon's testimony? (vv. 41–42) • What did the people think had happened to the king? (v. 43)	**mercy:** compassion; forgiveness; giving someone a second chance even when they might not deserve it

The gospel of Jesus Christ brings us joy.

KING LAMONI IS CONVERTED

OBJECTIVE

To help children learn that the gospel of Jesus Christ brings us joy.

BACKGROUND

Ammon taught King Lamoni (a Lamanite king) about God and the gospel. King Lamoni believed all that Ammon taught him and was so overcome with the spirit that he fell to the ground. The queen and all the people who were there thought that the king was dead.

GOSPEL ART PICTURE KIT

Unavailable

WORD QUEST

- sepulchre
- prostrate
- rebuked
- administered

VERSES	SUGGESTED QUESTIONS	TREASURES OF KNOWLEDGE
Alma 19:1–5	• What were the servants going to do with King Lamoni's body? (v. 1) • Why did the queen send for Ammon? (v. 5) • Why did some people think the king was dead? (v. 5)	**sepulchre:** a place where people are buried
Alma 19:6–8	• What was happening to King Lamoni? (v. 6) • What did Ammon tell the queen? (v. 8)	
Alma 19:9–11	• Why did Ammon say the queen was blessed? (v. 10)	
Alma 19:12–14	• What did the king say when he awoke? (v. 12) • What had the king seen while he was sleeping? (v. 13) • Why did the king, queen, and Ammon fall to the ground? (vv. 13–14)	
Alma 19:15–17	• What happened to the servants? (v. 16) • How did Abish know about the Lord? (v. 16) • What did Abish do when she saw all those that had fallen? (v. 17)	**prostrate:** lying flat, face down
Alma 19:18–20	• What did the people think had happened to those who had fallen? (vv. 19–20)	**rebuked:** criticized
Alma 19:21–24	• What happened to the Lamanite who tried to kill Ammon? (v. 22) • Why couldn't he kill Ammon? (v. 23) • How did the people feel after seeing the Lamanite fall dead? (v. 24)	

VERSES	SUGGESTED QUESTIONS	TREASURES OF KNOWLEDGE
Alma 19:25–28	• The people were arguing about why this had happened. What were some of their reasons? • Why was Abish sad? (v. 28)	
Alma 19:29–32	• What did the queen say when she arose? (v. 29) • What did the king say after he arose? (v. 31) • How did the people respond to the king's teachings? (vv. 31–32)	
Alma 19:33–36	• What happened to those who had fallen? (vv. 33–34) • What did the believers do? (v. 35) • Who does God "pour out his Spirit" upon? (v. 36)	**administered:** taught

Why is it important to make and keep covenants with the Lord?

THE ANTI-NEPHI-LEHIES

OBJECTIVE

To help children learn about the importance of making and keeping covenants with the Lord.

BACKGROUND

After King Lamoni and his people were converted, King Lamoni's father, king of all the Lamanites, learned about the gospel from Aaron. Aaron was one of Ammon's brothers who also went on a mission to the Lamanites. The Lamanite king accepted the gospel and was also converted.

GOSPEL ART PICTURE KIT

311: The Anti-Nephi-Lehies Burying Their Swords

WORD QUEST
- consecrating
- arms
- vouching
- idleness
- forbear
- stung
- zeal
- abhorrence

VERSES	SUGGESTED QUESTIONS	TREASURES OF KNOWLEDGE
Alma 23:1, 4–5	• What did the proclamation that the king sent out say? (v. 1) • What did Aaron and his brothers do? (v. 4) • How many Lamanites believed the teachings of Aaron and his brothers? (v. 5)	**consecrating:** dedicating to a sacred purpose
Alma 23:16–18	• Why did they want to have a different name? (v. 16) • What was the new name the converts chose for themselves? (v. 17) • What type of people were the Anti-Nephi-Lehies? (v. 18)	See comment about the name "Anti-Nephi-Lehies" at the end of the lesson.
Alma 24:1–2	• Who was angry with the Anti-Nephi-Lehies? (v. 1) • How did the rest of the Lamanites respond to the Anti-Nephi-Lehies? (vv. 1–2) • Why do you think the Amulonites and Amalekites encouraged the Lamanites to be angry at the Anti-Nephi-Lehies?	**arms:** weapons of war See "Who's Who" in the appendix for an explanation of the Amalekites and Amulonites. Jerusalem was a Lamanite city named after the city in Israel.
Alma 24:6, 17–18	• What did the Anti-Nephi-Lehies do with their weapons of war? (v. 17) • Why did they bury their weapons? (v. 18) • What did they covenant with the Lord? (v. 18)	**vouching:** testifying **idleness:** laziness

VERSES	SUGGESTED QUESTIONS	TREASURES OF KNOWLEDGE
Alma 24:19–22	• What was the purpose of the Lamanites going to war against the Anti-Nephi-Lehies? (v. 20) • What did the Anti-Nephi-Lehies do when the Lamanites came to battle against them? (vv. 21–22) • Why do you think they would rather die than fight?	
Alma 24:23–25	• How did some of the Lamanite warriors feel after killing the Anti-Nephi-Lehies and what did they do? (vv. 24–25)	**forbear:** stop **stung:** felt bad for what you had done
Alma 24:26–27	• What happened to those who were slain? (v. 26) • How many Lamanites joined the Anti-Nephi-Lehies that day? (v. 27)	
Alma 27:4–5, 14–16	• How did Ammon and his brothers feel about what was happening to the Anti-Nephi-Lehies? (v. 4) • What did Ammon and his brothers do for the Anti-Nephi-Lehies? (vv. 5, 14) • When arriving in Zarahemla, who did Ammon meet? (v. 16)	Ammon and Alma were friends. Ammon and his brothers were with Alma when the angel appeared (see Mosiah 27).
Alma 27:20–22	• What did the Nephites do for the Anti-Nephi-Lehies? (v. 22)	
Alma 27:26–30	• What did the Nephites call the Anti-Nephi-Lehies after arriving in Jershon? (v. 26) • What kind of people were the Anti-Nephi-Lehies? (vv. 27–30)	**zeal:** passion, enthusiasm **abhorrence:** a feeling of disgust

No one is certain why the converted Lamanites called themselves Anti-Nephi-Lehies. Joseph Fielding McConkie and Robert Millet suggest two possibilities. The word anti could have meant "opposed to or against," which would represent "a desire to dissolve barriers between Nephites and Lamanites, and thus establish peace."

Another possibility is that the word anti could have meant "like" or "mirror image," which would indicate their "desire to be as Nephi and Lehi of old" (Joseph Fielding McConkie and Robert L. Millet, *Doctrinal Commentary on the Book of Mormon, Vol. 3* [Salt Lake City: Bookcraft, 1991], 165).

You can gain a testimony by desiring it and by keeping the commandments.

GAINING A TESTIMONY

OBJECTIVE

To help children learn that they can gain a testimony of God's word by having a desire in their hearts and by keeping the commandments.

BACKGROUND

Alma went on a mission to preach to the Zoramites, a group of Nephites who separated themselves from the Church. The rich Zoramites would not allow the poor to worship in their churches. They were very prideful and rejected Alma's teachings. But the poor Zoramites had been humbled by their circumstances and were willing to listen.

GOSPEL ART PICTURE KIT

Unavailable

WORD QUEST
- arouse your faculties
- enlighten
- scorcheth
- barren
- long-suffering

VERSES	SUGGESTED QUESTIONS	TREASURES OF KNOWLEDGE
Alma 32:21, 26–27	• How does Alma define faith? (v. 21) • What does Alma say we need to do in order to obtain faith? (v. 27)	**arouse your faculties:** have a desire to learn
Alma 32:28–29	• What does Alma compare the "word" to? (v. 28) • What does he say we should do with the seed? (v. 28) • How will you feel if the seed is good? (v. 28)	The "word" refers to the word of God—the teachings of the gospel. **enlighten:** to give knowledge; to teach
Alma 32:30–32	• How can you tell if a seed is good? (v. 30) • How can you tell if a seed is not good? (v. 32) • How can we compare this to finding out if the gospel is true?	You can know the word of God is true by the way you feel inside when you obey the commandments, and by the blessings you begin to receive.
Alma 32:33–36	• How will you feel when you have a perfect knowledge of something? (v. 34) • If something is light, it is what? (v. 35) • When you plant the seed, what are you trying to find out? (v. 36)	
Alma 32:37, 41	• What will the tree bring forth after it gets root? (v. 37) • How do we nourish the tree? (v. 41)	

VERSES	SUGGESTED QUESTIONS	TREASURES OF KNOWLEDGE
Alma 32:38–40	• What happens when the sun comes up? (v. 38) • If the tree dies because of neglect, does that mean the seed was bad? (v. 39) • What will we not receive if we don't "nourish the word"? (v. 40) • Do you ever feel like you are neglecting your testimony? What are some changes you can make to begin nourishing your testimony?	**scorcheth:** burn **barren:** unable to reproduce Just like with the tree, we must not neglect our testimonies. If we stop praying, obeying the commandments, reading the scriptures, and learning about the gospel, we will begin to lose our testimonies.
Alma 32:42–43	• Describe the fruit. (v. 42) • What is the reward for taking care of the tree? (vv. 42–43)	**long-suffering:** continuing to be faithful and patient through trials The fruit represents eternal life (see page 11 for an explanation of eternal life).

After reading these verses, summarize what was taught to be sure your family understands what Alma was teaching: To gain a testimony, we need to first have the desire to know if the gospel is true. Then we need to nourish the seed we planted by obeying the commandments, studying the scriptures, praying, and so forth. If we have faith and patience, and keep doing all we're supposed to do, then our seed will grow into a testimony that can be strong like a tree. And one day we will receive eternal life—the greatest of all gifts.

We must pray to Heavenly Father daily to gain spiritual strength.

THE IMPORTANCE OF PRAYER

OBJECTIVE
To help children understand the importance of prayer and the reasons they need to pray.

BACKGROUND
Nephi and Alma taught important truths about prayer. When Jesus visited the Nephites, he taught them how to pray, and showed them through his example.

GOSPEL ART PICTURE KIT
605: Young Boy Praying

WORD QUEST
- grieveth
- welfare
- counsel
- hypocrite
- heathen
- amen

VERSES	SUGGESTED QUESTIONS	TREASURES OF KNOWLEDGE
2 Nephi 32:8–9	• What does the "evil spirit" (Satan) teach us about prayer? (v. 8) • Do you ever feel like not praying? • Why do you think Satan would not want you to pray? • How often should we pray? (v. 9) • In whose name should we pray? (v. 9)	**grieveth:** to feel sorrow
Alma 34:17–25	• Name seven things Alma says we need to pray for. • Discuss why each one of these is important and why we should pray for it.	
Alma 34:26–27	• How do you "pour out your soul"? • Do we have to pray in our closets? What do you think this actually means? • Why do you think we should pray for other people?	**welfare:** happiness or well-being If our hearts are "full, drawn out in prayer continually," we will think of Heavenly Father and Jesus and try to make the right choices.
Alma 37:37	• What should we do before we go to bed and when we wake up? • Do you "counsel with the Lord in all [your] doings"? • What does Alma tell us the Lord will do for us if we ask him for help?	**counsel:** to consult, talk with

VERSES	SUGGESTED QUESTIONS	TREASURES OF KNOWLEDGE
3 Nephi 13:5–8	• Who should we not be like when we pray? (v. 5) • How do the hypocrites pray? (v. 5) • What should we do when we pray? (vv. 6–7) • Do you use vain repetitions in your prayers?	**hypocrite:** someone who acts righteous but really isn't **heathen:** someone who does not believe in God Vain repetitions means to say the same things each time we pray without being meaningful and sincere. Even though God knows what we need before we ask, it is the act of asking that is important. Asking helps us to become humble, and it shows that we know we need God.
3 Nephi 13:9–13	• To whom should we pray? (v. 9) • Whose will do we pray to know and accept? (v. 10) • Should we forgive those who have hurt or offended us? (v. 11) • Can we expect help in times of temptation? (v. 12)	**amen:** an expression of approval or agreement
3 Nephi 14:7–11	• If we sincerely ask God for help, what will happen? (vv. 7–8) • What do verses 9–11 teach us about Heavenly Father's love for each of us?	" 'If ye then, being evil' is a reference to man's mortal and unsaved condition."* Jesus has given us a promise that our prayers will be answered. We need to trust the Lord. He loves us and will provide us with both our spiritual and temporal needs.

* Joseph Fielding McConkie, Robert L. Millet, and Brent L. Top, *Doctrinal Commentary on the Book of Mormon, Vol. 4* (Salt Lake City: Bookcraft, 1992), 92.

Liberty and free-dom are blessings from God. They're worth fighting for!

CAPTAIN MORONI AND THE TITLE OF LIBERTY

OBJECTIVE

To help children learn that liberty and freedom are blessings from God and worth fighting for.

BACKGROUND

A wicked man named Amalickiah wanted to be king of the Nephites living in Zarahemla during the time that captain Moroni was the head of the Nephite army, and Helaman (son of Alma the Younger) was the head of the Church. Moroni knew that if Amalickiah became king, Amalickiah would take away the people's freedom.

GOSPEL ART PICTURE KIT

312: Captain Moroni Raises the title of liberty

WORD QUEST

- dissensions
- rent
- girded
- loins
- liberty
- forsake
- hoisted

VERSES	SUGGESTED QUESTIONS	TREASURES OF KNOWLEDGE
Alma 45:20–22	• Why was it important to teach the people the word of God? (v. 21) • What did Helaman and his brethren do, and where did they go? (v. 22)	**dissensions:** disagreements
Alma 45:23–24	• Why wouldn't some of the people obey the teachings of Helaman? (v. 24)	
Alma 46:1–3	• What did those who didn't obey Helaman want to do to him? (v. 2) • What was the name of their leader? (v. 3)	
Alma 46:4–6	• What was Amalickiah's desire? (v. 4) • Who were the people who supported Amalickiah? (v. 4) • What did Amalickiah promise those who would support him? (v. 5)	
Alma 46:11–13, 16	• Who was Moroni, and how did he feel toward Amalickiah? (v. 11) • What did Moroni write on the torn piece of his coat? (v. 12) • What name did Moroni give to the written words on his torn coat? (v. 13) • What did Moroni pray for? (vv. 13, 16)	**rent:** tore **girded:** secured **loins:** part of the body between the ribs and the hips **liberty:** freedom

VERSES	SUGGESTED QUESTIONS	TREASURES OF KNOWLEDGE
Alma 46:17–20	• What did Moroni name the lands? (v. 17) • What did Moroni do with the title of liberty? (v. 19) • What did Moroni say to the people? (v. 20)	
Alma 46:21–22	• How did the people respond to what Moroni had asked them to do? (v. 21) • What did the tearing of their clothes mean? (v. 21) • What covenant did they make with God? (v. 22) • Have you made any covenants with God? Are you keeping them?	**forsake:** abandon
Alma 46:28–29	• Who did Moroni gather together? (v. 28) • What were the followers of Amalickiah called? (v. 28) • Why didn't Amalickiah and his followers want to fight? (v. 29) • Where did they go? (v. 29)	
Alma 46:30–33	• Why didn't Moroni want Amalickiah to join with the Lamanites? (v. 30) • What did Moroni and his army do? (v. 31–32) • Who was Moroni able capture, and where did he take them? (v. 33)	

VERSES	SUGGESTED QUESTIONS	TREASURES OF KNOWLEDGE
Alma 46:34–37	• What happened to the Amalickiahites who would not support the cause of freedom? (v. 35) • Did most of the Amalickiahites make the covenant of freedom? (v. 35) • Where did Moroni put the title of liberty, and what did it represent? (v. 36) • Why is freedom so important? What do you think it means to be free? • Do you think freedom is worth fighting for? Can you name some times in history when people have had to fight to protect their freedom? • How can we show our gratitude to those who have helped our nation become free?	**hoisted:** raised

HELAMAN AND THE TWO THOUSAND STRIPLING WARRIORS

God will protect you if you are obedient and have faith in Him.

OBJECTIVE

To help children learn that if they are obedient and have faith in God, He will protect them and keep them safe from their enemies.

BACKGROUND

After Ammon converted many of the Lamanites to the gospel, they took an oath to never fight again. The converted Lamanites went to live with the Nephites, where they could be protected from the wicked Lamanites. Many years later the wicked Lamanites started a war with the Nephites.

GOSPEL ART PICTURE KIT

313: Two Thousand Young Warriors

WORD QUEST
- bore
- stripling
- sally forth
- stratagem
- snare

72

VERSES	SUGGESTED QUESTIONS	TREASURES OF KNOWLEDGE
Alma 53:10–12	• What was the oath the converted Lamanites made? (v. 11) • Why did they go to live with the Nephites? (vv. 11–12)	
Alma 53:13–15	• Why did they want to fight again? (v. 13) • Why didn't Helaman want them to break their oath? (v. 15)	**bore:** carried
Alma 53:16–19	• Why were the sons able to take up arms against the Lamanites? (v. 16) • What was the covenant that the sons made? (v. 17) • How many young men decided to go to war? (v. 18)	
Alma 53:20–22	• What kind of young men were they? (vv. 20–21) • Who led the two thousand soldiers (v. 22)?	**stripling:** young man To "walk uprightly before God" means to be a good, honest person.
Alma 56:27–29	Note: The following verses are from a letter that Helaman sent to Moroni recounting the events of the war that took place. • What did the fathers of the sons bring to them? (v. 27) • Why were the Lamanites afraid? (v. 29)	**sally forth:** a sudden movement

VERSES	SUGGESTED QUESTIONS	TREASURES OF KNOWLEDGE
Alma 56:30–33	• What was Antipus's plan? (vv. 30–31) • What did Antipus' army do? (v. 33)	**stratagem:** a plan to surprise the enemy
Alma 56:34–37	• What did the Lamanite army do? (v. 35) • Whose army was marching behind the Lamanites? (v. 37) • Why did the Lamanites only want to march straight ahead? (v. 37)	
Alma 56:38–41	• Why did Helaman's army continue to move forward? (v. 39)	
Alma 56:42–44	• What happened in the morning of the third day? (v. 42) • What did Helaman ask his "sons"? (v. 44)	**snare:** trap
Alma 56:45–48	• How did the two thousand warriors respond to Helaman's question to them? (v. 46) • What had their mother's taught them? (v. 47)	
Alma 56:49–51	• What was happening to the army of Antipus?	
Alma 56:52–54	• What did the Lamanite army do when Helaman's army showed up? (v. 52) • What happened to the Lamanites after Helaman and his army joined the battle? (v. 54)	
Alma 56:55–57	• Did any of the two thousand young warriors die? (v. 56) • Why do you think all of them were saved?	

Having courage during adversity can bring great blessings.

NEPHI AND LEHI ARE SAVED IN PRISON

OBJECTIVE

To help children learn that having courage in the face of adversity can bring great blessings.

BACKGROUND

Nephi and Lehi were the sons of Helaman (see "Chart of Nephite Leaders" in the appendix). Nephi was the chief judge in Zarahemla but gave up the judgment seat so he and his brother Lehi could preach the gospel to the Nephites and Lamanites.

GOSPEL ART PICTURE KIT

Unavailable

WORD QUEST

- dumb
- dissenters
- overshadowed
- tumultuous
- disperse
- asunder
- bidden

VERSES	SUGGESTED QUESTIONS	TREASURES OF KNOWLEDGE
Helaman 5:18–20	• What did the Lord give Nephi and Lehi to help them in preaching the gospel? (v. 18) • How many Lamanites were converted? (v. 19) • Where did Lehi and Nephi go after Zarahemla? (v. 20)	
Helaman 5:21–23	• What did the Lamanite army do to Nephi and Lehi? (v. 21) • What prison were they kept in? (v. 21) • When the Lamanites went in to kill Nephi and Lehi, what did they find? (v. 23) • Why do you think they were encircled by fire? (v. 23)	
Helaman 5:24–27	• What did Nephi and Lehi say to the people? (v. 26) • What happened to the earth and the walls of the prison? (v. 27)	**dumb:** unable to speak **dissenters:** people who no longer want to be a part of a particular group
Helaman 5:28–30	• What were they overshadowed by? (v. 28) • What did the voice say to the multitude? (v. 29) • How did the voice sound? (v. 30)	**overshadowed:** covered **tumultuous:** loud
Helaman 5:31–34	• How many times did the voice speak to them, and what did it say? (vv. 32–33) • What happened to the earth and the walls when the voice spoke? (v. 33) • Why couldn't the Lamanites run away? (v. 34)	**disperse:** disappear **asunder:** apart

VERSES	SUGGESTED QUESTIONS	TREASURES OF KNOWLEDGE
Helaman 5:35–38	• What were Nephi and Lehi doing, and what did their faces look like? (v. 36) • What did the man tell the multitude to do? (v. 37)	
Helaman 5:39–42	• Who were Nephi and Lehi talking with? (v. 39) • How could the cloud of darkness be removed from the Lamanites? (v. 41) • What happened when the multitude prayed to God? (v. 42)	
Helaman 5:43–45	• What happened after the cloud of darkness dispersed? (v. 43) • What kind of feelings did the multitude experience while the fire surrounded them? (vv. 44–45)	
Helaman 5:46–48	• What did the people hear? (v. 47) • What did the people see when they looked up? (v. 48)	"Well Beloved" refers to Jesus Christ. If we have faith in him, and follow his ways, we will have peace and joy.
Helaman 5:49–52	• After this experience, what did the people go and do? (v. 50) • Were they able to convert others to the truth? (v. 50) • How did the converted Lamanites change? (vv. 51–52)	**bidden:** commanded

SAMUEL THE LAMANITE PROPHESIES OF CHRIST

If you have faith, God will give you strength beyond your abilities.

OBJECTIVE

To help children learn that if they have faith and trust in God, He can give them courage and strength beyond their own abilities.

BACKGROUND

In 6 BC a number of the Nephites had become very wicked, except for a few believers. However, many of the Lamanites were righteous and believed in God. Nephi, the son of Helaman, was the prophet at this time in the land of Zarahemla.

GOSPEL ART PICTURE KIT

314: Samuel the Lamanite on the Wall

WORD QUEST

- cast
- glad tidings
- rent in twain
- yield up the ghost

VERSES	SUGGESTED QUESTIONS	TREASURES OF KNOWLEDGE
Helaman 13:1–4	• Who was wicked and who was righteous at this time? (v. 1) • Why did the Nephites throw Samuel out? (v. 2) • Why did Samuel return to Zarahemla? (v. 3) • How did Samuel get back into the city so he could continue to warn the people? (v. 4)	**cast:** throw
Helaman 13:5–7	• What did Samuel say to the people from the top of the city wall? (v. 5) • What did Samuel prophesy would happen in four hundred years? (v. 5) • How could the people stop this destruction from happening? (v. 6)	**glad tidings:** good news If the "sword of justice falleth upon this people," they will be cut off from God's divine protection and destroyed by their enemies. Unfortunately, this is what happened to the Nephites (see Mormon 8:6–7).
Helaman 14:2–4	• What did Samuel prophesy would happen in five years? (v. 2) • What did Samuel say would happen the night before Christ was born? (vv. 3–4)	
Helaman 14:5–8	• What sign did Samuel give in verse 5? • According to Samuel's prophecy, how will the people react when they see the signs? (v. 7) • What will happen to those who believe in (and follow) the Son of God? (v. 8)	Everlasting life is synonymous with eternal life (see page 11 for an explanation).

VERSES	SUGGESTED QUESTIONS	TREASURES OF KNOWLEDGE
Helaman 14:20–22	• What signs did Samuel say would happen when Christ died? (v. 20) • How long would it be dark? (v. 20) • What did Samuel say would happen to the earth? (vv. 21–22)	**rent in twain:** torn in half **yield up the ghost:** to die (When Jesus yielded up the the ghost, His body and spirit separated.)
Helaman 14:23–27	• Name five signs that Samuel prophesied would take place when Christ died.	
Helaman 16:1–3	• When Samuel finished speaking from the city wall, what did the people who believed him do? (v. 1) • How did those who did not believe him react? (v. 2) • Were they able to hurt Samuel? Why not? (v. 2)	
Helaman 16:6–8	• Why did the wicked people think they couldn't hurt Samuel? (v. 6) • Where did Samuel go, and what did he do after he cast himself down from the wall? (v. 7)	

Many terrible events occurred in America when Jesus died in Jerusalem.

SIGNS OF CHRIST'S DEATH

OBJECTIVE

To teach children about the events that occurred on the American continent when Jesus Christ died in Jerusalem.

BACKGROUND

Many of the leaders of the Nephites were corrupt and did not believe in Jesus Christ. Some of the leaders were so angry that they wanted to kill the prophets and those who taught about Jesus. Nephi, the son of Nephi (see "Chart of Nephite Leaders"), was the prophet and leader of those who believed. He preached and baptized many of the Nephites.

GOSPEL ART PICTURE KIT

Unavailable

WORD QUEST

- just
- reckoning
- vapor
- mourning
- howling

VERSES	SUGGESTED QUESTIONS	TREASURES OF KNOWLEDGE
3 Nephi 8:1–4	• Why do you think you have to be cleansed from your iniquities before you can perform miracles? (v. 1) • What year was it? (v. 2) • What was the sign the people were looking for? (v. 3) • What began to happen among the people? (v. 4)	**just:** fair **reckoning:** calculation The Nephites changed how they measured time after the sign of Christ's birth was given. They had previously measured their time from when Lehi left Jerusalem (3 Nephi 2:6–8).
3 Nephi 8:5–7	• What was the date that the great storm began? (v. 5) • What are some of the disasters that occurred? (vv. 6–7)	
3 Nephi 8:8–11	• What happened to the cities of Zarahemla, Moroni, and Moronihah?	
3 Nephi 8:12–16	• Name five terrible things that happened in the land northward.	
3 Nephi 8:17–19	• What changes occurred "upon the face of the whole earth"? (vv. 17–18) • How long did the storms last? (v. 19) • What happened when the storms stopped? (v. 19)	

VERSES	SUGGESTED QUESTIONS	TREASURES OF KNOWLEDGE
3 Nephi 8:20–22	• Why weren't the people able to create any light? (v. 22) • What were the people not able to see? (v. 22)	**vapor:** mist
3 Nephi 8:23–25	• How long did the darkness last? (v. 23) • What were the people sad about, and what did they say? (vv. 24–25)	**mourning:** sadness **howling:** loud crying

After Jesus Christ was resurrected, He visited the American continent.

JESUS CHRIST APPEARS TO THE NEPHITES

OBJECTIVE

To help children learn about the resurrected Jesus Christ and His visit to the American continent.

BACKGROUND

In AD 34 all the signs of Christ's death that the prophets had testified of had come to pass. The righteous people who were not destroyed gathered at the temple in the land of Bountiful.

GOSPEL ART PICTURE KIT

315: Jesus Christ Appears to the Nephites
316: Jesus Teaching in the Western Hemisphere
317: Jesus Healing the Nephites
322: Jesus Blesses the Nephite Children

WORD QUEST

- steadfastly
- wist
- hosanna
- ponder
- tarry
- bowels
- halt
- sufficient

VERSES	SUGGESTED QUESTIONS	TREASURES OF KNOWLEDGE
3 Nephi 11:1–4	• Where were the people gathered? (v. 1) • What did the people hear, and where did it come from? (v. 3) • What did the voice sound like? (v. 3) • How did the people feel when they heard the voice? (v. 3)	
3 Nephi 11:5–7	• How many times did they hear the voice? (v. 5) • What did the voice say? (v. 7) • Who do you think was speaking? • What other times in the scriptures has Heavenly Father introduced Jesus Christ?	**steadfastly:** constantly
3 Nephi 11:8–11	• Who came down from heaven? (v. 10) • What did He look like, and what did He say to the people? (vv. 8, 10–11)	**wist:** knew Jesus is the source of all life and light, and "all men must look to him for these things."*
3 Nephi 11:12–15	• What did Christ allow the multitude to do? (v. 14) • Why do you think He did this? (v. 15)	Christ's ascension (rising) into heaven occurred on the fortieth day after his resurrection in Jerusalem.
3 Nephi 11:16–17	• What did the people say and do after touching Christ? (v. 17) • How do you think you would have felt if you had been there?	**hosanna:** "save now, save we pray"**

* Bruce R. McConkie, *Mormon Doctrine.* 2d ed. (Salt Lake City: Bookcraft, 1979), 447.
** Joseph Fielding McConkie, Robert L. Millet, and Brent L. Top, *Doctrinal Commentary on the Book of Mormon, Vol. 4* (Salt Lake City: Bookcraft, 1992), 53.

VERSES	SUGGESTED QUESTIONS	TREASURES OF KNOWLEDGE
3 Nephi 17:1–3	• What did Jesus ask the people to go home and do? (v. 3) • Why do you think it's important to think about the teachings of Jesus? • Jesus said we can ask Heavenly Father to help us understand His teachings. Do you need help understanding some of Jesus' teachings?	**ponder:** think about
3 Nephi 17:4–6	• Where was Jesus going to go after leaving the Nephites? (v. 4) • How did the multitude react when Jesus told them He had to leave? How did this make Jesus feel? (vv. 5–6)	**tarry:** remain **bowels:** emotions "The lost tribes of Israel" refers to the ten tribes of Israel who were taken captive into Assyria (a nation to the north) in 721 BC. No one (except God) knows where they went after that—which is why they are referred to as being "lost."
3 Nephi 17:7–10	• Describe some of the people Jesus healed. (v. 9) • What did the people do after Jesus healed the sick? (v. 10)	**halt:** crippled; lame **sufficient:** enough
3 Nephi 17:11–13	• What did Jesus ask the people to do? (v. 11) • What did Jesus and the children do? (v. 12)	

VERSES	SUGGESTED QUESTIONS	TREASURES OF KNOWLEDGE
3 Nephi 17:23–25	• Who came down from heaven? (v. 24) • What did they do? (v. 24) • How do you think you might have felt if you were one of the children there? • How many people were there? (v. 25) • What can you do in your life now to prepare yourself so that you can be with Jesus when He comes again?	

When you take the sacrament, you renew your baptismal covenants.

THE SACRAMENT

OBJECTIVE

To help children understand the purpose and importance of the sacrament.

BACKGROUND

When Jesus Christ appeared to the Nephites, He called twelve men to be Apostles. He set them apart and gave them authority to teach his gospel and to perform sacred ordinances for the people.

GOSPEL ART PICTURE KIT

603: Blessing the Sacrament
604: Passing the Sacrament

WORD QUEST
- disciple
- administering
- sanctify

VERSES	SUGGESTED QUESTIONS	TREASURES OF KNOWLEDGE
3 Nephi 18:1–4	• What did Jesus ask His disciples to do? (v. 1) • What did Jesus do with the bread? (v. 3)	**disciple**: a follower of Jesus; in this verse it refers to the Nephite apostles called by Jesus Christ (3 Nephi 19:4)
3 Nephi 18:5–7	• Who should the sacrament be given to? (v. 5) • What does the bread represent? (v. 7)	
3 Nephi 18:8–11	• What did Jesus give to the multitude after the bread? (v. 8) • What does the wine (or water) represent? (v. 11) • What does Jesus promise us if we always remember Him? (v. 11) • What are the blessings that come from having His Spirit with us?	Joseph Smith was told in a revelation not to use wine in the sacrament, so today we use water (see D&C 27:2–3).
Moroni 4:1–3	• Who can bless and pass the sacrament? (v. 1) • Does this scripture sound familiar? (v. 3) Where have you heard this prayer before? • Name three things we promise to do when we partake of the bread. (v. 3)	**administering**: blessing **sanctify**: to make holy
Moroni 5:1–2	• What and whom should we remember when we drink the water? (v. 2) • Next time you hear the sacrament prayers, listen to them carefully and remember that the prayer was given to us by Jesus. • What are some things you can think of to help you remember Jesus next time you take the sacrament? • When else should we remember Jesus? What can you do to help you remember Him more? • (Optional) Read through the sacrament prayers one sentence at a time and discuss the meaning of each sentence with your family.	

MORMON—A GREAT MAN OF GOD

Mormon was a great spiritual man and military leader.

OBJECTIVE

To help children learn about the prophet Mormon, a great spiritual man and military leader, who abridged the records of the Nephites and wrote the book of Mormon.

BACKGROUND

In the year AD 321, Ammaron, the keeper of all the plates that had been passed down for generations since the time of Lehi, was commanded by the Lord to hide the sacred records in a hill. Two hundred eighty-eight years had passed since Christ had visited the Nephites, and there was much wickedness among the people of Nephi.

GOSPEL ART PICTURE KIT

319: Mormon Bids Farewell to a Once Great Nation

WORD QUEST
- sober
- prevail
- willfully
- sorceries

VERSES	SUGGESTED QUESTIONS	TREASURES OF KNOWLEDGE
Mormon 1:1–4	• What did Mormon call his record? (v. 1) • How old was Mormon when Ammaron told him about the plates? (v. 2) • Why did Ammaron choose Mormon to become the next keeper of the plates? (v. 2) • Which plates did Ammaron tell Mormon to take, and what was he supposed to write on them? (v. 4)	**sober:** serious; disciplined
Mormon 1:5–7	• What was Mormon's father's name, and who was he a descendant of? (v. 5) • Where did Mormon and his father move when Mormon was eleven years old? (v. 6)	
Mormon 1:8–10	• What were the names of the groups who were considered Nephites? (v. 8) • What were the names of the groups who were considered Lamanites? (v. 9) • Who were these groups of people descendants of? • Why do you think they were still fighting with one another after all those years?	
Mormon 1:11–13	• Who won the battle between the Nephites and the Lamanites? (v. 11) • How long was there peace in the land after the battle ended? (v. 12) • Why did the Lord take away the disciples from the Nephites? (v. 13)	**prevail:** to triumph or win The term "beloved disciples" refers to the three Nephite apostles who asked to remain on the earth as translated beings to minister and preach until the second coming of Jesus Christ (see 3 Nephi 28).

VERSES	SUGGESTED QUESTIONS	TREASURES OF KNOWLEDGE
Mormon 1:14–15	• Why didn't the Nephites have the Holy Ghost with them anymore? (v. 14) • Will the Holy Ghost stay with us when we are not living righteously? • Who visited Mormon when he was fifteen years old? (v. 15) • What kind of boy do you think Mormon was?	President Joseph Fielding Smith taught that "the Holy Ghost will not dwell with that person who is unwilling to obey and keep the commandments of God or who violates those commandments willfully."* (See also Helaman 4:24–25.)
Mormon 1:16–17	• Why was Mormon not allowed to preach to the Nephites? (v. 16) • How wicked do you think the Nephites were if the Lord didn't want the gospel preached to them?	**wilfully:** done on purpose
Mormon 1:18–19	• What happened to the treasures of the Nephites? (v. 18) • Who had power over the hearts of the people? (v. 19) • (Optional) Read Samuel the Lamanite's prophecy of the Nephites' destruction in Helaman 13:5–20 and Abinadi's prophecy in Mosiah 12:8.	**sorceries:** the power of commanding evil spirits
Mormon 2:1–2	• What was Mormon appointed to do when he was sixteen years old? (v. 1)	

* *Book of Mormon Student Manual.* 2d ed. Salt lake City: The Church of Jesus Christ of Latter-day Saints, 1982, 43

THE DESTRUCTION
OF THE NEPHITES

The Lord's Spirit cannot dwell with the wicked.

OBJECTIVE

To help children learn the importance of living righteously and how the Lord and His Spirit will not dwell with people if they are wicked.

BACKGROUND

In the year AD 327, Mormon was sixteen years old and was asked to be the leader of the Nephite armies. For the next thirty-four years, he led the Nephites in many battles against the Lamanites. During this period, the Nephites took possession of the land northward, and the Lamanites possessed the land southward.

GOSPEL ART PICTURE KIT

Unavailable

WORD QUEST

- avenge
- utterly
- manifest
- epistle
- hewn
- midst
- molder
- incorruptible bodies

VERSES	SUGGESTED QUESTIONS	TREASURES OF KNOWLEDGE
Mormon 3:7–10	• Who won the battle between the Nephites and the Lamanites? (vv. 7–8) • Why did the Nephites "begin to boast"? (v. 9) • What did the Nephites decide to do that was wrong? (v. 10) • Why do you think it's wrong to seek revenge? What should you do when someone has hurt you?	**avenge:** to hurt or harm someone because they hurt you. Desolation was a Nephite city located north of the land of Bountiful.
Mormon 3:11–13	• Why did Mormon decide to not be a leader anymore? (v. 11) • What does Mormon write that demonstrates his love for his people? (v. 12)	**utterly:** completely
Mormon 3:14–16	• Why wouldn't God protect the Nephites anymore? (v. 15) • What did Mormon do after he stopped leading the Nephite army? (v. 16)	**manifest:** reveal
Mormon 4:16–18	• How many Lamanites came down to battle against the Nephites? (v. 17) • Did the Nephites win any more battles after this time? (v. 18)	
Mormon 4:22–23	• Where did Mormon go, and why? (v. 23) • Why do you think it was important for him to take all the records?	

VERSES	SUGGESTED QUESTIONS	TREASURES OF KNOWLEDGE
Mormon 5:1–2	• Did Mormon decide to help the Nephites again? (v. 1) • Why was Mormon without hope? (v. 2) • What does verse 2 teach us about the importance of repentance and prayer?	
Mormon 6:1–4	• What did Mormon ask the Lamanite king, and what was the King's response? (vv. 2–3) • Where did the Nephites gather for the final battle? (v. 4)	**epistle:** a letter
Mormon 6:5–6	• What would the Lamanites have done to the sacred records if they had found them? (v. 6) • Where did Mormon hide the records? (v. 6) • What plates did he give to Moroni? (v. 6)	
Mormon 6:7–11	• Why were the Nephites afraid? (v. 7) • What happened to Mormon in the final battle? (v. 10) • How many Nephites survived the battle? (v. 11)	**hewn:** cut **midst:** the center
Mormon 6:12–15	• How many Nephites were with each leader? • Approximately how many Nephites died in the battle?	**molder:** to crumble to dust
Mormon 6:16–19	• Why was Mormon filled with sorrow? (v. 16) • What would have happened to the Nephites if they had not rejected Jesus? (v. 17)	

VERSES	SUGGESTED QUESTIONS	TREASURES OF KNOWLEDGE
Mormon 6:20–22	• What will happen to our bodies after we die? (v. 21) • When we stand before the judgement-seat of Christ after we are resurrected, how will we be judged? (v. 21) • What have you learned by studying about the destruction of the Nephites?	**incorruptible bodies:** immortal, resurrected bodies

The Lord is concerned about your problems and will help you solve them.

THE BROTHER OF JARED

OBJECTIVE

To help children learn that the Lord is concerned with their problems and will help them find solutions to them.

WORD QUEST
- dash
- veil

BACKGROUND

A righteous man named Jared lived during the time of the Tower of Babel—approximately 2200 BC (see Genesis 11:1–9). When the Lord changed the languages of the people, Jared asked his brother to pray to the Lord not to change the language of their families. The Lord answered his prayers and led them to the promised land. This happened many hundreds of years before Lehi and his family left Jerusalem. However, the Jaredites were still living in the promised land (in a different location) even after Lehi's family arrived.

GOSPEL ART PICTURE KIT

318: The Brother of Jared Sees the Finger of the Lord

VERSES	SUGGESTED QUESTIONS	TREASURES OF KNOWLEDGE
Ether 2:13–15	• What did the Jaredites call the name of the place where they stayed, and how long did they stay there? (v. 13) • Why do you think the Lord was upset with the brother of Jared? (v. 14) • Why do you think prayer is so important? • Are we able to have the Lord's Spirit with us when we sin? (v. 15)	Joseph Smith taught that the name of the brother of Jared was Mahonri Moriancumer.*
Ether 2:16–17	• The barges were light like ____ (v. 16) and tight like ____. (v. 17) • How long were the barges? (v. 17)	
Ether 2:18–21	• What were some of the problems the brother of Jared needed the Lord's help with? (v. 19) • What did the Lord tell him to do? (v. 20)	
Ether 2:22–25	• What was the brother of Jared worried would happen while they were crossing the ocean? (v. 22) • Why couldn't they have windows? (v. 23) • Who controls the winds and the rains? (v. 24) • What did the Lord ask the brother of Jared? (v. 25)	**dash:** beat
Ether 3:1, 4–5	• How many barges were built? (v. 1) • How many stones did the brother of Jared make? (v. 1) • What did the stones look like? (v. 1) • What did the brother of Jared ask the Lord to do? (v. 4)	

* McConkie, Bruce R. *Mormon Doctrine.* 2d ed. Salt Lake City: Bookcraft, 1979 463.

VERSES	SUGGESTED QUESTIONS	TREASURES OF KNOWLEDGE
Ether 3:6–8	• What did the brother of Jared see? (v. 6) • What did the finger of the Lord look like? (v. 6) • How did the brother of Jared react when he saw the finger of the Lord? (v. 6) • Why was the brother of Jared afraid when he saw the Lord's finger? (v. 8)	**veil:** a separation between our mortal world and the heavens
Ether 3:9–13	• Why was the brother of Jared allowed to see the finger of the Lord? (v. 9) • Is God capable of lying? (v. 12) • How does knowing God cannot lie make you feel? • Because of his great faith, what more was the brother of Jared able to see? (v. 13)	
Ether 3:25–28	• What did the Lord show to the brother of Jared? (v. 25) • What did the Lord tell the brother of Jared to do? (v. 27)	The two stones that the Lord gave the brother of Jared were the Urim and Thummim, an instrument Joseph Smith used to translate the Book of Mormon (see D&C 17:1).
Ether 6:2–4	• What did the brother of Jared do with the stones? (v. 2) • What did the people take with them in the barges? (v. 4)	
Ether 6:5–7	• What did God cause the wind to do? (v. 5) • What was traveling to the promised land like? (vv. 6–7) • Why didn't the great waves hurt them? (v. 7)	

VERSES	SUGGESTED QUESTIONS	TREASURES OF KNOWLEDGE
Ether 6:8–10	• How often did they give thanks to the Lord? (v. 9) • Why do you think they were so grateful? • In what ways did the Lord help them on their journey? (vv. 8, 10)	
Ether 6:11–13	• How long was their journey upon the water? (v. 11) • What did they do when they arrived in the promised land? (vv. 12–13)	

To gain a testimony of the Book of Mormon, you need to read, ponder, and pray.

MORONI'S PROMISE

OBJECTIVE

To help children learn how to gain a testimony of the Book of Mormon.

BACKGROUND

All of the Nephites except Moroni (son of Mormon) were destroyed by the Lamanites in AD 400. Before Mormon died, he gave Moroni the gold plates (the abridged record of the Nephite people). Moroni then wandered alone for about twenty years. During that time he abridged the plates of the Jaredites (the book of Ether) and added his own writings to the gold plates before he finally buried them.

GOSPEL ART PICTURE KIT

306: Mormon Abridging the Plates
320: Moroni Hides the Plates in the Hill Cumorah

WORD QUEST

- intent
- kinsfolk
- ministered

VERSES	SUGGESTED QUESTIONS	TREASURES OF KNOWLEDGE
Mormon 8:1–3	• What happened to the Nephites who escaped the destruction at the last battle? (v. 2) • What happened to Mormon? (v. 3)	
Mormon 8:4–6	• What did Moroni do with the records? (v. 4) • Did any of Moroni's friends or family survive the battle? (v. 5) • Why do you think Moroni was spared? • How would you feel if you were Moroni?	**intent:** purpose **kinsfolk:** relatives
Mormon 8:7–9	• After the Nephites were all destroyed, did the Lamanites stop fighting? (v. 8) • Who was left among this once great nation of people? (v. 9)	
Mormon 8:10–12	• Was there anyone left except Moroni who knew and worshipped God? (v. 10) • Where did the disciples of Jesus go after they left the Nephites? (v. 10) • Who did the disciples minister to? (v. 11)	**ministered:** gave service

VERSES	SUGGESTED QUESTIONS	TREASURES OF KNOWLEDGE
Moroni 10:1–5	• What does Mormon tell us to remember? (v. 3) • What does Moroni tell us to do after we read the Book of Mormon? (v. 3) • When we pray to know if the Book of Mormon is true, we should ask with _____ (name three things). (v. 4) How can we do each of these? • How will we know if the Book of Mormon is true? (vv. 4–5) • Read the quote by Ezra Taft Benson in the "Treasures of Knowledge" column and discuss why it's important for each person to gain a testimony of the Book of Mormon. • Challenge each member of the family to follow Moroni's counsel and find out for themselves if the Book of Mormon is true. This would also be a good opportunity for members of the family to discuss their feelings about the Book of Mormon, and for those who have a testimony to share it with the others.	President Ezra Taft Benson explained the importance of gaining a testimony of the Book of Mormon. He said, "The Book of Mormon is the keystone of our religion. [A keystone is the central stone in an arch. It holds all the other stones in place, and if removed, the arch crumbles.] It is the keystone of our witness of Christ. It is the keystone of our doctrine. It is the keystone of testimony. . . . "There is a power in the book which will begin to flow into your lives the moment you begin a serious study of the book. You will find greater power to resist temptation. You will find the power to avoid deception. You will find the power to stay on the strait and narrow path."*

*Conference Report, October 1986.

APPENDIX

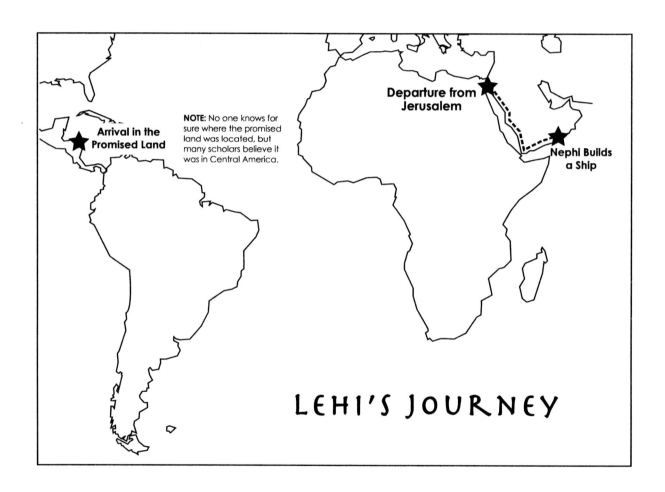

Departure from Jerusalem

Nephi Builds a Ship

Arrival in the Promised Land

NOTE: No one knows for sure where the promised land was located, but many scholars believe it was in Central America.

LEHI'S JOURNEY

NEPHITE LEADERS

Lehi
|
Nephi
|
THE NEPHITES

LAND OF ZARAHEMLA

Mosiah
|
King Benjamin
|
Mosiah II
|
Ammon

Alma
|
Alma
|
Helaman
|
Helaman
|
Nephi & Lehi
|
Nephi
(Apostle of Jesus)
|
Amos
|
Ammaron
|

LAND OF NEPHI-LEHI

Zeniff
|
Noah   Abinadi
|
Limhi

Capt. Moroni
Stripling Warriors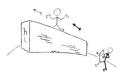

Samuel the Lamanite

Mormon
|
Moroni

BOOK OF MORMON CITIES AND OCCUPANTS

This page explains the major Nephite cities discussed in the study guide. It can be used with the map below as a reference to help children visualize where events happened. It can also be studied as a topic with the included scriptural references. (Please note that the map shows the *possible* sites for the cities. No one is certain where they were actually located.)

1. The Land of **Nephi** was where Nephi and his descendants lived up until the reign of the Nephite king Mosiah I. The Lord commanded Mosiah to take all those who believed in the Lord and to leave the land of Nephi (see Omni 1:12).

2. Mosiah and his followers discovered the land of **Zarahemla**, where the Mulekites were living. (The Mulekites left Jerusalem and came to the promised land just like Nephi and his family.) The Mulekites and the people of Mosiah lived together, and Mosiah became their king (see Omni 1:14–19).

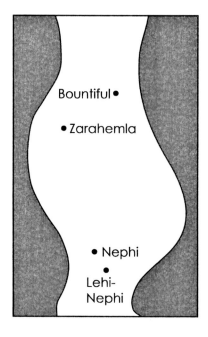

3. During the reign of Mosiah I, a man named Zeniff took a group of people back to the land of **Nephi** (see Omni 1:27–30).

The Lamanite king allowed Zeniff and his people to live in the city of **Lehi-Nephi**, but they were put into bondage (see Mosiah 7:21–22).

Many years later, under the reign of King Limhi, the Nephites escaped from the Lamanites and returned to the land of Zarahemla.

4. The land of **Bountiful** was where Jesus Christ appeared to the people on the American continent.

WHO'S WHO IN THE BOOK OF MORMON

Do you sometimes forget a person's name who we've studied? Do you ever read about somebody but can't remember where they lived or what they did? The following section can help you to better know the people in the Book of Mormon stories that are in this guide. Each description includes when and where that person lived, along with a brief highlight of their lives. Check the timeline at the bottom of the page to get an idea of what time period each person lived in.

AARON
100 BC—Zarahemla and Lamanite lands
Aaron was one of the sons of King Mosiah. He rebelled against the Church along with his brothers and Alma the Younger. He was later converted when an angel appeared to Alma. He went on a mission to the Lamanites and converted the king of the Lamanites to the gospel.

ABINADI
150 BC—Lehi-Nephi
Abinadi was a prophet who was sent to preach repentance to King Noah and his followers. The king and his priests rejected Abinadi's teachings and burned him to death.

ALMA (THE ELDER)
150 BC—Lehi-Nephi and Zarahemla
Alma was one of the priests of King Noah. He believed the teachings of Abinadi and established the church of Christ among the believers. He and his followers were discovered by the Lamanites and were put under bondage. With God's help, they later escaped to the land of Zarahemla, where Alma became the high priest of the Church during the reign of King Mosiah II.

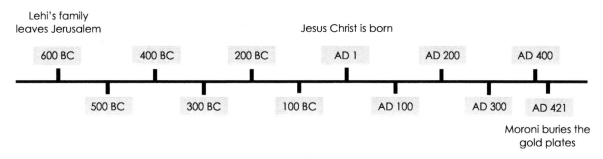

Lehi's family leaves Jerusalem

Jesus Christ is born

600 BC   500 BC   400 BC   300 BC   200 BC   100 BC   AD 1   AD 100   AD 200   AD 300   AD 400   AD 421

Moroni buries the gold plates

ALMA (THE YOUNGER)
100 BC—Zarahemla
Alma was the son of Alma the Elder. He and the sons of King Mosiah rebelled against the Church. They were visited by an angel and converted to the gospel of Jesus Christ. Alma became the high priest after his father died and was also the first chief judge. He later gave up the position of chief judge to preach the gospel to the Nephites. The book of Alma bears his name.

AMALEKITES
90 BC—Lamanite lands
The Amalekites were a group of Nephites who left and joined with the Lamanites. They fought against the Anti-Nephi-Lehies and the Nephites.

AMALICKIAH
50 BC—Zarahemla and Lamanite lands
Amalickiah desired to be king of the Nephites and to take away their freedom. But he was chased out of Zarahemla by Captain Moroni, who wrote the title of liberty. Amalickiah joined up with the Lamanites and later became their king.

AMMON (1)
121 BC—Zarahemla and Lehi-Nephi
Ammon was the leader of a group who went to the land of Nephi to find the people of Zeniff. He was put into prison by King Limhi but was later released when the king discovered Ammon was a Nephite. Ammon helped King Limhi and his people escape from the bondage of the Lamanites.

AMMON (2)
100 BC—Zarahemla and Lamanite lands
Ammon was one of the sons of King Mosiah. He went on a mission to the Lamanites for fourteen years. He cut off the arms of some wicked Lamanites to show his faithfulness as a servant of the king. He taught the gospel to King Lamoni and many other Lamanites who joined the Church.

AMMON, PEOPLE OF
(See ANTI-NEPHI-LEHIES)

AMULON
150 BC—Lehi-Nephi and Helam
Amulon was one of the wicked priests of King Noah. When the Lamanites attacked their city, the priests fled into the wilderness. While hiding in the wilderness, they kidnapped Lamanite women and married them. Amulon and the priests were later discovered by the Lamanites and joined with them. The Lamanite king appointed Amulon to be a ruler of Alma (the Elder) and his people, who were living in the land of Helam.

AMULONITES
90 BC—Lamanite lands
Amulonites were followers and descendants of Amulon. They joined with the Lamanites and fought against the Anti-Nephi-Lehies and Nephites.

ANTI-NEPHI-LEHIES
90 BC—Lamanite lands and land of Jershon
The Anti-Nephi-Lehies (also known as the people of Ammon) were a group of Lamanites who were taught the gospel by Ammon and his brothers. They repented of their sins and buried all their weapons of war. They later moved to the Nephite land of Jershon and were protected by the Nephites. Their sons became the two thousand stripling warriors.

ANTIPUS
65 BC—Zarahemla
Antipus was a leader in the Nephite army. He fought a battle against the Lamanites with the help of Helaman and the two thousand stripling warriors.

BENJAMIN (KING)
130 BC—Zarahemla
Benjamin was the son of Mosiah I. He became the king of Zarahemla after his father died. He preached his last sermon to the Nephite people atop a tower so they could hear his voice.

BROTHER OF JARED
2200 BC—Tower of Babel and promised land
Mahonri Moriancumer was the brother of Jared. He lived during the time of the Tower of Babel. He asked the Lord to touch sixteen stones for light in their barges. He and his family sailed to the promised land hundreds of years before Lehi's family.

GIDEON
145 BC—Lehi-Nephi and Zarahemla
Gideon was a strong Nephite who did not like King Noah. Later, Gideon helped develop a plan for King Limhi and his people to escape from the Lamanites and return to Zarahemla. When he was older, he fought against and was killed by a wicked man name Nehor. A valley and a city were named after Gideon.

HELAM
145 BC—Waters of Mormon
Helam was the first person baptized by Alma the Elder at the Waters of Mormon. Helam was the name of the city where Alma (the elder) and his followers lived and were in bondage to the Lamanites.

HELAMAN
74 BC—Zarahemla
Helaman was the son of Alma the Younger. He was a high priest in the Church and was the leader of the two thousand stripling warriors.

HELAMAN II
53 BC—Zarahemla
Helaman was the son of Helaman. He was the chief judge in the land. The book of Helaman bears his name.

HIMNI
100 BC—Zarahemla and Lamanite lands
Himni was one of the sons of King Mosiah. He rebelled against the Church along with his brothers

and Alma the Younger. He was later converted when an angel appeared to Alma. He went on a mission to the Lamanites for fourteen years.

ISHMAEL
600 BC—Jerusalem

Ishmael and his family joined Lehi and his family in the wilderness. His daughters married Lehi's sons. Ishmael died in the wilderness. His sons and their descendants were called Ishmaelites and were part of the Lamanites.

JACOB
599 BC—Wilderness of Judea to the promised land

Jacob was one of the sons of Lehi. He was born while they were traveling in the wilderness. Before Nephi died, he gave the records of his family to Jacob. The book of Jacob bears his name.

JARED
2200 BC—Tower of Babel and promised land

Jared lived during the time of the Tower of Babel. His brother was a prophet of God. He and his family sailed to the promised land hundreds of years before Lehi's family.

JOSEPH
595 BC—Wilderness of Judea to the promised land

Joseph was one of the sons of Lehi. He was born while they were traveling in the wilderness.

LABAN
600 BC—Jerusalem

Laban was the keeper of the brass plates. Nephi and his brothers tried to get the brass plates from him, but he wouldn't give them the plates. Nephi was commanded to kill Laban.

LAMAN
600 BC—Jerusalem to the promised land

Laman was the eldest son of Lehi. He often rejected the teachings of his father and Nephi. He later rebelled against God, and his descendants were part of the Lamanites.

LAMONI
90 BC—Land of Ishmael

Lamoni was a Lamanite king who became converted to the gospel of Jesus Christ through the teachings of Ammon.

LEHI
600 BC—Jerusalem to the promised land

Lehi was a prophet of God who lived in Jerusalem. God commanded him to take his family and leave Jerusalem. He was shown many visions, like the tree of life. He and his family traveled in the wilderness for many years and then sailed to the promised land.

LEHI
45 BC—Zarahemla

Lehi was the son of Helaman II. He and his brother

Nephi went on a mission to teach the Lamanites and were put in prison. They were saved by God and the prison walls fell down.

LEMUEL
600 BC—Jerusalem to the promised land
Lemuel was one of the son's of Lehi. He often rejected the teachings of his father and Nephi. He later rebelled against God, and his descendants were part of the Lamanites.

LIMHI
121 BC—Lehi-Nephi
Limhi was the son of King Noah. He and his people were in bondage to the Lamanites until they were able to escape with the help of Ammon.

MORMON
AD 333—Zarahemla
Mormon was the prophet who wrote the Book of Mormon by abridging the records of the Nephites. He was the leader of the Nephite army and died at the last battle between the Nephites and Lamanites. The book of Mormon bears his name.

MORONI
74 BC—Zarahemla
Moroni was the chief captain of all the Nephite armies. He believed in freedom and helped maintain it in the Nephite lands. He wrote the title of liberty and helped fight many battles against the Lamanites.

MORONI
AD 421
Moroni was the son of Mormon. He was the last record keeper and last survivor of the Nephites. He buried the gold plates and appeared as an angel to Joseph Smith in 1823. The book of Moroni bears his name.

MOSIAH I (KING)
200 BC—Land of Nephi and Zarahemla
Mosiah, a descendant of Nephi, was commanded to take the followers of God and leave the land of Nephi. They discovered the land of Zarahemla and the people living there. Mosiah became their king.

MOSIAH II (KING)
100 BC—Zarahemla
Mosiah was the son of King Benjamin. His sons and Alma the Younger rebelled against the Church, but they were later converted after an angel appeared. The book of Mosiah bears his name.

MULEK
589 BC—Jerusalem to the the promised land
Mulek was a son of King Zedekiah in Jerusalem. He escaped the destruction of Jerusalem, and the Lord brought him and his people to the promised land. His descendants lived in the land of Zarahemla when King Mosiah I and his followers joined them.

NEPHI (1)
600 BC—Jerusalem to the promised land
Nephi was one of the sons of Lehi. He was a great

prophet and follower of God. He returned to Jerusalem to get the brass plates from Laban. He built the ship that his family sailed in to get to the promised land. He was the keeper of the records and a leader over his people. The first and second books of Nephi bear his name.

NEPHI (2)
45 BC—Zarahemla

Nephi was the son of Helaman II. He was a great prophet among the Nephites. He and his brother Lehi went on a mission to teach the Lamanites and were cast into prison. They were saved by God and the prison walls fell down. He baptized those in Zarahemla who believed the teachings of Samuel the Lamanite.

NEPHI (3)
AD 1—Zarahemla and Bountiful

Nephi was the son of Nephi (2). He was called by Jesus to be one of the twelve Nephite disciples. The third book of Nephi bears his name. The fourth book of Nephi is named after his son.

NOAH
160 BC—Lehi-Nephi

Noah was the king of the Nephites living in the land of Lehi-Nephi. He was a wicked king who rejected the teachings of Abinadi. He ordered Abinadi to be burned to death. King Noah was later burned to death by his own people.

OMNER
100 BC—Zarahemla and Lamanite Lands

Omner was one of the sons of King Mosiah. He rebelled against the Church along with his brothers and Alma the Younger. He was later converted when an angel appeared to Alma. He went on a mission to the Lamanites for fourteen years.

SAM
600 BC—Jerusalem to the Land of Promise

Sam was one of the sons of Lehi. He believed the teachings of his father and Nephi. He went with Nephi to Jerusalem to get the brass plates from Laban.

SAMUEL THE LAMANITE
6 BC—Zarahemla

Samuel was a Lamanite prophet who was sent to Zarahemla to preach repentance to the Nephites. He also prophesied of the birth and death of Jesus Christ. He taught the people from atop the city wall. Those who were angry tried to kill him, but they were unable to and Samuel safely escaped.

SARIAH
600 BC—Jerusalem to the Land of Promise

Sariah was the wife of Lehi. She traveled out of Jerusalem with her family through the wilderness and sailed across the ocean to the promised land.

SONS OF MOSIAH
100 BC—Zarahemla and Lamanite lands
The sons of King Mosiah II were Ammon, Aaron, Omner, and Himni.

ZARAHEMLA
200 BC—Zarahemla
Zarahemla was a descendant of Mulek. Zarahemla was the leader of the people living in the land of Zarahemla at the time Mosiah I discovered them.

ZENIFF
200 BC—Lehi-Nephi
Zeniff was a Nephite who left Zarahemla and returned to the land of Nephi. The Lamanite king allowed the Nephites to live in the city of Lehi-Nephi, but they were put into bondage by the Lamanites. Zeniff was the father of King Noah and grandfather to King Limhi.

ZORAM
600 BC—Jerusalem to the Land of Promise
Zoram was the servant of Laban. He took an oath with Nephi and went with Lehi's group into the wilderness. He married one of Ishmael's daughters and sailed with Lehi and his family to the promised land.

WORD QUEST GLOSSARY

Finding new words and learning their meanings can be exciting and helpful in understanding the scriptures. **_Keep track of the new words you have discovered by writing down the definitions in your own words_**. You will often come upon these words again while reading other sections of the Book of Mormon. If you've forgotten their definitions, you can easily look them up here in the Word Quest Glossary. Enjoy your search!

abhorrence (p. 60):

abominations(p. 27)

administered (p. 57):

administering (p. 89):

affliction (p. 44)

amen (p. 67):

and it came to pass (p. 2):

apprised (p. 36):

arms (p. 59):

arouse your faculties (p. 63):

asunder (p. 76):

authority (p. 35):

avenge: (p. 94):

bade (p. 9):

barren (p. 64):

bellows (p. 17):

bidden (p. 77):

boast (p. 23):

boldness (p. 38):

bondage (p. 27):

bore (p. 73):

bowels (p. 86):

broken heart (p. 32):

burden (p. 34):

cast (p. 79):

ceasing (p. 48):

chastened (p. 14):

chasten (p. 42):

commence (p. 11):

concourses (p. 11):

condemn (p. 25):

confound (p. 2):

consecrating (p. 59):

constrained (p. 8):

contend (p. 50):

contrite spirit (p. 32):

counsel (p. 66):

countenance (p. 53):

covenant (p. 34):

covet (p. 25):

cunning (p. 44):

curious workmanship (p. 14):

dash (p. 98):

descendant (p. 28):

diligent (p. 9):

disciple (p. 89):

disperse (p. 76):

despitefully use (p. 32):

dissensions (p. 69):

dissenters (p. 76):

dumb (p. 76):

durst (p. 2):

dwindle (p. 8):

endeavor (p. 38):

enlighten (p. 63):

epistle (p. 95):

exhorted (p. 41):

expound (p. 54):

exquisite (p. 48):

faggots (p. 29):

faith (p. 14):

favor (p. 44):

flattery (p. 47):

forbear (p. 60):

forefathers (p. 5):

forsake (p. 70):

glad tidings (p. 79):

girded (p. 69):

graven images (p. 31):

grieveth (p. 66):

grievous to be bourne (p. 38):

guile (p. 54):

guiltless (p. 31):

hallowed (p. 31):

halt (p. 86):

hardness of their hearts (p. 3):

harrowed up (p. 47)

haste (p. 45):

hearkened (p. 39):

heathen (p. 67):

heed (p. 14):

hereafter (p. 44):

hewn (p. 95):

hilt (p. 8):

hither (p. 5):

hither and thither (p. 8):

hitherto (p. 39):

hoisted (p. 71):

hosanna (p. 85):

howling (p. 83):

humble (p. 20):

hypocrite (p. 67):

idleness (p. 59):

idolatrous (p. 47):

incorruptible bodies (p. 96):

indebted (p. 24):

iniquities (p. 6):

intent (p. 102):

just (p. 82):

kinsfolk (p. 102):

lest (p. 9):

liberty (p. 69):

loins (p. 69):

long-suffering (p. 64):

lowliness of heart (p. 3):

manifest (p. 94):

mercy (p. 54):

mete (p. 32):

midst (p. 95):

ministered (p. 102):

molder (p. 95):

molten (p. 17):

mourn (p. 34):

mourning (p. 83):

murmur (p. 2):

notwithstanding (p. 53):

oath (p. 9):

ordained (p. 35):

ore (p. 17):

overshadowed (p. 76):

persecute (p. 44):

plunder (p. 44):

ponder (p. 86):

prevail (p. 91):

proclamation (p. 39):

prophesy (p. 27):

prosper (p. 3):

prostrate (p. 56):

racked (p. 47):

rebuked (p. 56):

reckoning (p. 82):

redemption (p. 34)

rent (p. 69):

rent with anguish (p. 18):

rent in twain (p. 80):

remission (p. 25):

repent (p. 24):

resorted thither (p. 34):

resurrection (p. 34):

sally forth (p. 73):

sanctify (p. 89):

sepulchre (p. 56):

scorcheth (p. 64):

scourged (p. 29):

sheath (p. 8):

sin (p. 25):

slew (p. 51):

slothful (p. 15):

smite (p. 6):

snare (p. 74):

sober (p. 91):

soberness (p. 20):

sojourn (p. 17):

sorceries (p. 92):

sore (p. 20):

stature (p. 3):

steadfastly (p. 85):

stiffneckedness (p. 2):

stratagem (p. 74):

stripling (p. 73):

stung (p. 60):

subjects (p. 39):

succor (p. 24):

suffered (p. 23):

sufficient (p. 86):

swift to do iniquity (p. 18):

swollen (p. 50):

tarry (p. 86):

teasings (p. 38)

tempest (p. 20):

thereof (p. 11):

timbers (p. 20):

transgress (p. 24):

tribute (p. 38):

tumultuous (p. 76):

unprofitable servant (p. 24):

utterly (p. 94):

vain (p. 24):

vapor (p. 83):

visionary (p. 2):

veil (p. 99):

vouching (p. 59):

wade (p. 17):

waxed (p. 23):

welfare (p. 66):

whit (p. 8):

whither (p. 11):

whoredoms (p. 27):

willfully (p. 92):

wist (p. 85):

wo (p. 25):

wroth (p. 8):

wrought (p. 18):

yea (p. 2):

yield up the ghost (p. 80):

zeal (p. 60):

SCRIPTURE STRIPS

Instructions: Cut out the titles below and place in a container. Each time you gather for Scripture Study let someone choose which story to read by picking a title from the container.

LEHI'S FAMILY LEAVES JERUSALEM

THE BRASS PLATES I

THE BRASS PLATES II

THE TREE OF LIFE

THE LIAHONA

NEPHI BUILDS A SHIP

TRAVELING TO THE PROMISED LAND

KING BENJAMIN'S TEACHINGS ON SERVICE

ABINADI'S COURAGE

THE COMMANDMENTS

ALMA BAPTIZES

THE PEOPLE OF LIMHI ESCAPE FROM BONDAGE

ALMA'S PEOPLE ARE PUT IN BONDAGE

ALMA'S PEOPLE ARE DELIVERED

ALMA THE YOUNGER

AMMON: MISSIONARY TO THE LAMANITES

AMMON TEACHES KING LAMONI

KING LAMONI IS CONVERTED

THE ANTI-NEPHI-LEHIES

GAINING A TESTIMONY

PRAYER

GAMES, GAMES, GAMES!

This section contains thirty-two fun family activities that are quick and easy to prepare. Activities are divided into three sections: activities that help increase comprehension by using questions from the lessons, activities that help reinforce Book of Mormon knowledge, and activities just for fun. There are a variety of games to meet the needs of both older and younger children. Enjoy!

ACTIVITIES TO HELP INCREASE COMPREHENSION

TESTIMONY SPIN

Object: Answer questions correctly.
Preparation: Bottle, questions from any lesson.

Sit in a circle. Take turns spinning the bottle. Whoever the bottle points to has to answer a question from the lesson. If they get the answer right, they can spin the bottle. If they get the answer wrong, the previous player spins the bottle again. Keep playing until all the questions have been answered.

RACE TO 25

Object: Answer questions correctly and roll the highest numbers.
Preparation: Dice, paper, pencil, questions from lesson.

Each person takes a turn rolling the dice. Whatever the dice lands on is how many points the question is worth. After the player rolls the dice, he or she attempts to answer a question. If the person answers the question correctly, he or she gets the points. Keep track of each person's points. The first person to get 25 points wins.

SPELLING BEE

Object: Be the first person to spell *pray*.
Preparation: Enough index cards or paper cut into squares so each family member will get four cards (if there are four people in your family, you'll need sixteen cards). On each card write one letter of the word *pray*. Make as many cards needed so that each family member can spell *pray*.

Place all the cards upside down on the table or floor. Have each person take turns answering questions from the lesson. If they get a question right, they can pick a card from the pile. If they pick a letter that they already have, they have to put the letter back and wait until their next turn to pick again. The first person to spell the word *pray* wins.

SEARCHING FOR ANSWERS

Object: "Catch" questions with a fishing pole and answer correctly.
Preparation: Fishing pole or stick, string, magnet, paper clips, sheet or blanket. Tie a long string to the

end of the stick and attach a magnet to the end of the string. Hang a blanket in front of the fishing pond. Write questions from the lesson on paper (paper can be cut in the shape of a fish) with a paper clip attached. Place the questions on the floor behind the blanket.

Each person in the family takes a turn going fishing by placing the fishing pole over the blanket and trying to catch a question. If they can answer the question right, they can keep their fish. If not, they have to put it back. Whoever gets the most fish wins. (To make the game more challenging for older children, write answers from questions on the fish. Ask each person a question and have them try to catch the right answer. If they don't catch the right answer, they have to put it back. Whoever gets the most fish wins.)

KNOCK AND RECEIVE

Object: Knock down bottles and receive points for questions answered correctly.

Preparation: Ten empty two-liter bottles, ball, ten pieces of paper, tape, questions from the lesson.

Line up the bottles like bowling pins at one end of the room on a hard surface. Each person takes a turn answering a question from the lesson. Each time a player answers a question correctly, they get to bowl for their points. The player receives one point for each bottle knocked over. Give each family member as many turns as you want. Keep track of each player's points and add them up at the end to see who wins! (Pair younger children with someone older and let the

younger child try to knock down the bottles while the older person answers the question.)

POP THE QUESTION

Object: Be the first person to find the answer to a question hidden in a balloon.

Preparation: Balloons, paper, and pencil. Write down questions from a lesson on a strip of paper. Be sure to include the scripture reference where the answer can be found. Roll up the paper, place in a balloon, and fill the balloon with air. (Do this for as many rounds as wanted.)

Toss the balloons on the floor and have each member of the family (or divide into teams with a mixture of older and younger children) race to pop a balloon, read the question inside, and find the answer in the scriptures (even if someone knows an answer, they still must find the answer in the scriptures). The first person (or team) to do this wins that round. Play as many rounds as wanted.

PAR-A-DICE

Object: Roll doubles, and collect the most question cards.

Preparation: Write down questions from the lesson (or you can use a variety of questions from past lessons as a review) on as many cards as wanted; pair of dice.

Sit in a circle and place question cards in the middle. Take turns rolling the dice. When someone rolls a double, they can choose a question from the pile. If they answer correctly, they keep the card. If not, they place the card at the bottom of the pile. Keep playing until all the cards are gone. Whoever has the most cards at the end wins.

AROUND THE PROMISED LAND

Object: Answer the most questions correctly and return to your original seat.

Set up chairs in a circle. Have one person sitting outside of the circle reading the questions from any lesson. Pick a person to start with. He or she stands up along with the person to their right. The person in charge reads a question from the lesson. Whoever answers first gets to continue on and the other person sits down. The next person to the right stands up with the person who got the answer correct on the previous question. The goal is to get back to your original seat. Whoever

answers incorrectly sits down in the seat of the person he or she was going against. Whoever gets back to their original seat wins.

POINT, SHOOT, SCORE

Object: Answer the question correctly, and land your airplane closest to the highest point card.

Preparation: Paper, questions from lesson, cards marked 1 pt, 5 pts, 10 pts, 25 pts.

Give each family member a piece of paper to make paper airplanes. Place the point cards around the room, with the lowest points being the closest to where you will stand to launch your airplane. Have someone read a question from the lesson. If it is answered correctly, the person can throw their airplane and try to hit (or get close to) a point card to earn points. The person with the most points wins.

GAMES THAT REINFORCE BOOK OF MORMON KNOWLEDGE

MORMON'S SCRIPTURE MATCH

Object: Be the first to match up verses and scriptural references.

Preparation: Write the following scripture phrases in one column and the scriptural references in another column on as many pieces of paper as needed for each family member or for each team to have one.

Scriptural Phrases

1. "I know that the Lord giveth no commandments . . . save he shall prepare a way."
2. "Behold, my beloved Son in whom I am well pleased"
3. "For God had commanded me that I should build a ship."
4. "And behold, all that he requires of you is to keep his commandments."
5. "I will not recall the words which I have spoken unto you . . . for they are true."
6. "I cried within my heart: O Jesus, thou Son of God, have mercy on me."
7. "Therefore if ye have faith ye hope for things which are not seen, which are true."
8. "Seek, and ye shall find."
9. "Yea, Lord, I know that thou speakest the truth . . . and canst not lie"
10. "And by the power of the Holy Ghost ye may know the truth of all things."

Scriptural References

A. Alma 32:21
B. Mosiah 2:22
C. 3 Nephi 14:7
D. 1 Nephi 3:7
E. Ether 3:12
F. Moroni 10:5
G. 1 Nephi 17:49
H. Alma 36:18
I. 3 Nephi 11:7
J. Mosiah 17:9

(Answers: 1. D; 2. I; 3. G; 4. B; 5. J; 6. H; 7. A; 8. C; 9. E; 10. F)

Give each family member or team a paper with the verses and references written on it, and a pencil. The first person or team to match them correctly wins! (Challenge: Have someone read a scriptural phrase out loud. Each person or team races to find it in their scriptures.)

QUICK GUESS

Object: Be the first person to guess the missing word from a scripture verse and earn the most points.

Materials: dice

Have one family member choose a verse from one of the lessons and read all but one word to the rest of the family. The first person to yell out the missing word correctly gets to roll the dice. Whatever number they roll is how many points they receive. Take turns reading verses. Keep track of points, and the person with the most points at the end wins. (For older children, leave out phrases instead of just a word. For younger children, let them look in their scriptures.)

MORMON'S BOOK

Object: Be able to name all the books in the Book of Mormon in order.

Have the family stand in a circle. Pick one person to start. Begin by naming the first book in the Book of Mormon (1 Nephi), the next person must name the next book. Take turns saying all the books in their proper order. If a family member says an incorrect book or doesn't know the answer, he or she sits down. Whoever says the last book (Moroni) wins that round. (Challenge for older children: Have one person say all the names in order as fast as they can. Whoever can name them all the fastest wins.)

TOSS AND TELL

Object: List facts about Book of Mormon characters.
Preparation: Tape names of Book of Mormon characters on a ball, so that the ball is covered with names. (see "Who's Who" for suggestions.)

Have the family stand in a circle. One person starts by tossing the ball to a family member. Whoever catches the ball must say one fact about the character written on the ball where their right thumb touches. (Example, if their right thumb touches the name Laman, they can say, "Nephi's brother".) If the person can't name a fact, they are out. Keep playing until there is only one person left.

FOUR CORNERS OF THE PROMISED LAND

Object: Match Book of Mormon characters with the books they are in, in the Book of Mormon.
Preparation: Write the following on cards: 1 Nephi, Mosiah, Alma, Helaman. Tape one card in each corner of the room. Write the following on cards or pieces of paper (the answers are in parentheses next to each name and can be written on the back of the card): Zoram (Nephi), Laman (Nephi), Lemuel (Nephi), Lehi (Nephi), Jacob (Nephi), King Benjamin (Mosiah), King Mosiah (Mosiah), Alma the Elder (Mosiah), Limhi (Mosiah), Noah (Mosiah), Abinadi (Mosiah), Alma the Younger (Mosiah or Alma), Ammon (Mosiah or Alma), King Lamoni (Alma), Anti-Nephi-Lehies (Alma), Helaman (Alma or Helaman), 2000 stripling warriors (Alma), Antipus (Alma), Gideon (Mosiah), Nephi and Lehi—the brothers (Helaman), Samuel the Lamanite (Helaman), Pahoran (Helaman), Nephi, son of Helaman (Helaman). (More names can be added.)

Have one person read a card. Each person decides which book they think that character is in. They then go and stand under the card they think is correct. The person in charge tells which corner is correct and the people in that corner get a point. Keep track of points earned. Take turns reading cards, and play until all cards are read. The person with the most points wins. (Challenge: Read verses from the scriptures and each person must stand under the name of the book where they think that verse is located.)

FIND THE TRUE MEANING
Object: Guess the correct meaning of a word.
Preparation: Write the following on index cards or paper: "yea: truly"; "and it came to pass: a way to connect thoughts or ideas"; "murmur: complain"; "iniquities: sins"; "bade: commanded"; "suffer: allow"; "chastened: corrected"; "hallowed: holy"; "mourn: to feel sorrow"; "proclamation: announcement." (More words and definitions can be added if needed by looking in the Word Quest glossary).

Give each member of the family a word card, and a pencil. Allow them a few minutes to look over their word and write down two other definitions that could go with the word (but are not correct). Each family member takes a turn reading their word and the three definitions (only one of which is correct). The family has to guess which definition is the correct one. If the person can trick the family into choosing the wrong definition, they get a point. Whoever gets the most points wins. (Adaptation for younger children: Have the parents read the word and two definitions: one right, one wrong. If the child guesses the correct definition they get a point.)

SCRIPTURE SCRAMBLER
Object: Be the first to unscramble a word and make as many new words with the given letters.

Preparation: Write the following on cards or paper (answers to scrambled words are in parentheses): eritohdops (priesthood); rnmomo (mormon); atnrele (eternal); gnlea (angel); maal (alma); secdelip (disciple); huffital (faithful); mlikihacaa (amalickiah); bmeremre (remember); thrayic (charity); dnmcomatmne (commandment); hysohltg (holy ghost); troammlytli (immortality); mihil (Limhi).

This game can be played a couple of ways. One way is to show each family member (or team) a card. The first person (or team) to unscramble the word, wins a point. Another way to play is to give each family member (or team) a piece of paper and pencil. Show them a card and have them write as many words as they can using those letters. They get a point for each word they can make, and extra points if they can guess the original scrambled word.

TWENTY QUESTIONS
Object: Guess a word by asking less than twenty yes-or-no questions.
Preparation: Write the following on strips of paper: brass plates, Liahona, Nephi, tree of life, Sariah, Ammon, Laban's sword, promised land. (You can add more words if needed.) Fold and place the strips of paper in a container.

Have one family member take a slip of paper. The rest of the family tries to guess what is written on their paper by asking questions that can be answered with a yes or no (For example: "Is it a person?" "Is it a place?"

"Is it a thing?") The family has to try and guess it by asking only twenty questions. Give each person a turn picking a slip of paper.

WHO AM I?
Object: Guess the names of Book of Mormon characters.

Preparation: Write the following names on a piece of paper: Nephi, King Benjamin, Ammon, Moroni, Laman, Alma the Younger, 2,000 Stripling Warriors, Samuel the Lamanite, Moroni (write more names if needed).

Tape the name of a character on each person's back. The object of the game is to guess what name is on your back by asking other family members yes-or-no questions.

BOOK OF MORMON CHARADES
Object: Guess the scene being acted out.

Preparation: Write the following (or choose your own) on strips of paper: Nephi builds a ship, Lehi's dream, Ammon slays the Lamanites, Mormon writes on the gold plates; King Benjamin preaches from a tower; Nephi's brothers tie him up; Alma the Younger is visited by an angel; Joseph Smith finds the gold plates. (More phrases can be added). Fold and place papers in a container.

Divide the family into two teams and have one member of each team pick a paper from the container and act out the scene with no talking. Each team gets a chance to guess first; if they can't guess correctly, the other team gets a chance to guess. The team who guesses the most phrases correctly, wins.

ABC BOOK OF MORMON
Object: Learn and remember words from the Book of Mormon.

One person starts with the letter *A* and says, "I'm reading the Book of Mormon and I see the word ____" and says a word from the Book of Mormon that starts with the letter *A*. Another member of the family then has to repeat what was just said and then says the same phrase but uses the letter *B*. The third family member says what the first two said, and then adds a word that begins with *C*. Keep going until someone can't remember all of the letters. (For younger children, don't have them repeat the previous letters and phrases, and allow them to look in their scriptures.)

LAST LETTER, FIRST LETTER
Object: Say a Book of Mormon word that begins with the same letter as the last word just said.

Choose someone to go first. They say any name or word from the Book of Mormon. The person to their right then says a word that begins with the last letter of the word just said. (For example: person one says Nephi, the person to their right could say Ishmael, the person to their right could say Lemuel, and so forth.) If someone cannot come up with a word, they are out. Keep going around the circle until there is only one person left. (To make it more challenging, give each person a time frame in which they must say their word. For younger children, allow them to use their scriptures.)

GAMES FOR FUN!

PARTAKE OF THE FRUIT

Object: Place your fruit closest to the tree.

Preparation: Large poster-size paper, cardstock or paper, crayons or markers, scissors, tape, and blindfold.

On a poster-size paper have the family help to draw a picture of Lehi's dream. Draw and color a piece of fruit on cardstock for each family member. Cut out the fruit and place a piece of tape on the back of each. Hang the poster of Lehi's dream on the wall and play "Pin the fruit on the tree." Blindfold and spin around a member of the family and have them try to place their fruit on the tree. Whoever gets the closest to the tree wins.

SEEK AND YE SHALL FIND

Object: Find the hidden ball.

Preparation: Ball, paper, tape, crayons or markers.

Have your family cover a ball with paper and decorate it to look like the Liahona. Have one family member leave the room while the other members hide the ball. When the family member returns have them look for the ball by following the clues the other family members give. One way to do this is to have the family hum or sing a Book of Mormon song. When the person gets close to the hidden ball, the family hums loudly. When the person is far away, they hum softly. Take turns letting each family member find the ball.

REMEMBER, REMEMBER

Object: Find matching Book of Mormon characters and phrases.

Preparation: Write the following on index cards or paper cut into squares: Nephi; Builds a ship; King Benjamin; Preaches from a tower; Alma; A priest of King Noah; Alma; The Younger; Ammon; Cuts off arms of enemies; Captain Moroni; title of liberty; Helaman; 2000 stripling warriors; Samuel; Preaches from a wall; Brother of Jared; Sees the Lord's finger; Moroni; Buries the gold plates.

Shuffle the cards and place them in rows upside down. Have each family member take turns turning two cards over. If they get a match, they keep the cards and take another turn. If they don't get a match, they turn both cards back over and their turn is over. Play until all cards have been matched. Whoever gets the most matches wins.

LET THE SPIRIT GUIDE YOU

Object: Find the ball while blindfolded.

Preparation: Ball, blindfold. Place chairs, toys, or other obstacles throughout the room.

Have family members take turns being blindfolded. Throw a ball into the middle of the room. First have the blindfolded person try to find the ball with some members of the family yelling out clues to help and others yelling out directions that are wrong. Next, have the blindfolded person try to find the ball with one family member walking next to them whispering directions in their ear, while other family members are yelling out right and wrong directions. When each person has had a turn, compare how much easier it was to find the ball with the help of a family member whispering correct instructions, instead of trying to listen to all the different voices. Compare it to getting through life with the help of the Holy Ghost to guide us.

RESTORATION RELAY

Object: Be the first team to find word matches.

Preparation: 40 Index cards or paper cut into cards. Write each of the following on four cards: faith, commandments, prayer, prophets, courage, service, love, eternal life, Holy Ghost, testimony. Divide the cards into four sets with each set having all ten words written on them.

Divide the family into two teams. Place two sets of cards at one end of the room, facedown on the floor. Have team members line up at the other side of the room, with each team receiving one set of cards. One member of each team picks a card, races to the other end of the room and picks one card from the floor. If it's a match, they take the card and return to their team at the end of the line. If the card is not a match, they place it back on the floor and return to their team at the back of the line, and try to match their card when they get to the front of the line again. The first team to match all of their cards wins.

NEPHITES, NEPHITES, LAMANITES

Play like Duck, Duck, Goose. The family sits down in a circle facing each other. One person is It and walks around the circle. As they walk around, they tap people's heads and say whether they are a Nephite or a Lamanite. Once someone is the Lamanite, they get up and try to chase It around the circle. The goal is to tap that person before they are able sit down in the Lamanite's spot. If the Lamanite is not able to do this, they become It for the next round and play continues. If they do tap the It, the person tagged has to be It again.

BOOK OF MORMON DRAW!

Object: Guess the word being drawn.

Preparation: Paper (large paper works best), pencil or pen. Write the following words on slips of paper: title of liberty, Laman and Lemuel, rod of iron, King Benjamin, ship, the Ten Commandments, sheep, Nephi's ship, praying, Ammon (more words can be added if needed).

Let one member of the family pick a slip of paper and draw a picture of the word. Give each person 60 seconds to draw clues for the family to guess, but they can't use letters or numbers in their drawing. Give each person a turn at drawing a picture. The game can also be played in teams, with only team members being allowed to guess the picture, and points given to the team if the picture is guessed within 60 seconds.

MORMON SAYS

Play like Simon Says. Pick one person to be Mormon and stand at the front of the room. Mormon will give directions for the family to follow (example: smile, read scriptures, pray, love your neighbor, sing "I am a Child of God," murmur). The family should only follow when the leader says "Mormon says". If a family member follows the directions when the leader does not say "Mormon says" they must sit down. The last person standing wins, and gets to be "Mormon". Give everyone a turn to be "Mormon".

FOLLOW THE PROPHET

Object: Listen to and follow the leader.
Preparation: Rope or long string, blindfolds.

Have everyone, except the leader, blindfolded or just close their eyes, and hold on to a rope. Have the leader hold on to one end of the rope and walk through the house or yard and lead the others by giving them directions ("take a step up the stairs," "turn left," "step over the toys," etc.). Let everyone have a turn being the leader. Afterwards, discuss the importance of following the prophet, who can see things that we can't. Just like Lehi's family had faith in their father as he led them out of Jerusalem, we need to have faith and follow our prophet today, and let him lead us back to our Heavenly Father.

NEPHITE DETECTIVE

Object: Be the first person to locate a word in the scriptures.

Give each person a set of scriptures (everyone must keep them closed). Let one person start by saying any word that can be found in the Book of Mormon. Everyone opens their scriptures and begins searching for that word. The first person to find it wins that round. Give everyone a turn at picking a word, and play as many rounds as wanted. For younger children, use words that can be found easily. For older children, use harder words that are not used as frequently.

BOOK OF MORMON MOVIE NIGHT

Object: Act out different scenes from the Book of Mormon.

Divide the family into groups (pair parents or older children with younger children). Pick a scene from the Book of Mormon (possible scenes: Nephi and his brothers get the brass plates; the tree of life; sailing to the promised land; King Benjamin's speech; Alma and the sons of King Mosiah see an angel; Ammon and the Lamanites, Nephi and Lehi are saved in prison; Jesus visits the Nephites). Have each group act out their scene with costumes and dialog. Give each group time to practice, find costumes, make a set, etc. Either act out for the family or record each scene and watch them all together like a movie.

ABOUT THE AUTHOR

Janet Burningham was born and raised in Provo, Utah. After graduating from BYU with a BS in elementary education, she taught elementary and middle school for several years. She has also developed curriculum for various educational programs, such as math and study skills. Currently she is a full-time mother.

Janet and her husband, Scott, are the parents of four children: Joshua, Katey, Madeline, and Benjamin.

Her hobbies include reading, writing, walking, enjoying the outdoors, and spending time with family and friends.

0 26575 71272 8